JAVA

Programming Basics

for the Internet

For use with Microsoft® Visual J++™ Ver. 1.1

E. Shane Turner

Karl Barksdale

Gary Ashton

Kal Bumgardner

Todd Knowlton

Eugene Paulsen

Earl Jay Stephens

JOIN US ON THE INTERNET
WWW: http://www.thomson.com
EMAIL: findit@kiosk.thomson.com   A service of I(T)P®

South-Western Educational Publishing
an International Thomson Publishing company I(T)P®

Cincinnati • Albany, NY • Belmont, CA • Bonn • Boston • Detroit • Johannesburg • London • Madrid
Melbourne • Mexico City • New York • Paris • Singapore • Tokyo • Toronto • Washington

Copyright © 1998

by SOUTH-WESTERN EDUCATIONAL PUBLISHING

Cincinnati, Ohio

ISBN: 0-538-68012-1

2 3 4 5 6 7 C1 03 02 01 00 99 98

Printed in the United States of America

Managing Editor: Carol Volz
Editor: Shannon O'Connor
Consulting Editor: Minta Berry
Marketing Manager: Stephen Wright
Art Coordinator: Mike Broussard
Production Services: Electro-Publishing
Internal Design: Ann Small

Library of Congress Cataloging-in-Publication Data
JAVA Programming Basics for the Internet / E. Shane Turner…[et al.].
          p.   cm.
     Includes Index.
     ISBN 0-538-68012-1
     1. Java (Computer program language)   I. Turner, E. Shane.
     QA76.73.J38J3598   1997
     005.2'762--dc21   97-31336
                                                         CIP

International Thomson Publishing

South-Western Educational Publishing is a division of International Thomson Publishing, Inc.
The ITP logo is a registered trademark used herein under license by South-Western Educational Publishing.

Contents

Preface

The Internet provides the most exciting new software development environment since the invention of the personal computer. The fastest growing part of the Internet is called the World Wide Web. The Web revolutionized the Internet by allowing pictures, sound, video, and other multimedia to be displayed and shared by Web enthusiasts.

Java has become the programming tool of choice for the Web. It allows Web pages to be viewed on different computer platforms. Java rides the Web in the form of little software programs called **applets**. Java allows a programmer to create applets and attach them to Web pages for display and execution on Web computers around the planet.

If you have surfed the Web, you have seen numerous Web pages. Many of the pages were created using Java applets. This book will introduce you to the exciting world of Java programming.

About *Java: Programming Basics for the Internet*

Java: Programming Basics for the Internet covers the essential use of Java on the World Wide Web. This book will show you how Java works and the basics of how to create your own Java applets using Microsoft's Visual J++ Developer Studio.

In this text you will learn to create applets and add them to your Web pages. The Microsoft Visual J++ software makes it easy to use Java. Visual J++ Developer Studio comes with Microsoft's Internet Explorer so you can test your Web applets after you create them.

If you are considering a professional programming career or if you want to be able to develop Web pages for your own use, Visual J++ will be an essential development tool. This introduction to Visual J++ provides a foundation for your continued exploration of this exciting tool.

What You Need to Use This Book

The following list details the required and recommended items needed to use this tutorial effectively:

Required:

• A copy of Microsoft's Visual J++
• Windows 95 or Windows NT 4.0 or higher (Internet Explorer accompanies Windows 95 and Windows NT.)
• A 486 processor minimum with 8MB of RAM and 20MB of free hard drive space. A Pentium processor with 12MB of RAM is preferred.

Since Java rides the Web, a basic understanding of the World Wide Web and of HTML would be helpful as you learn Java. The following texts from South-Western Educational Publishing can help you gain the necessary skills:

- *Internet Activities: Adventures on the Superhighway* 0-538-65147-4
- *HTML Activities: Webtop Publishing on the Superhighway* 0-538-67458-X

Book Organization

Java Programming Basics is divided into three skill-building sections:

Sector 1: Java Rides the Web searches for and explores examples of Java on the Web. This Sector explains how Java applets can be used and what problems Java can solve.

Sector 2: Building Java Applets with Visual J++ teaches you how to use the powerful Java development tools included in the Visual J++ development environment. You will install and use the Microsoft Visual J++ Developer Studio and create interesting applet projects, testing them with the Internet Explorer.

Sector 3: Applets on the Superhighway guides you as you build Web pages using Java applets.

This book follows a very simple, hands-on activity approach for ease of learning. You learn Java by using it to build applets and develop Web pages.

Frequent Illustrations

Frequent illustrations will help you visualize the steps required to complete the activities. A sample illustration is shown in Figure P.1. Callouts are used to introduce key parts on the computer screen. You can use the illustrations for reference as you complete the steps in the activity.

Figure P.1
Compiling your Java code
A – Click Save
B – Select Build Hello1
C – Watch your code compile

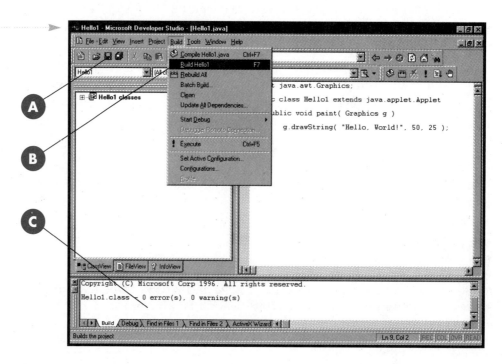

Step-by-Step Instructions

The activities contain a complete set of instructions. By following the instructions carefully, you will successfully complete each activity. The steps that accompany Figure P.1 are shown below.

 Step 1: To compile your code:

        1A: Click the **Save** button to save your changes.

        1B: Select *Build Hello1* from the **Build** menu.

        1C: Watch as your code compiles in the window marked in Figure P-1.

Comments, FAQs, and DEBUG Hints

To help you become proficient with Java, we have included Comments, Debug hints, and the answers to Frequently Asked Questions (FAQs):

 //**Comments** clarify difficult operations or give you alternative ways of accomplishing a task.

 FAQs: give you extra information to think about.

 DEBUG helps you find and solve problems.

Debriefings, List of Terms, and Challenges

Debriefings appear at the end of each chapter and activity. Debriefings provide summaries of activities. A list of new terms is found at the end of each chapter. Careful review of these terms will reinforce your understanding of the important concepts presented in the chapter. Many of the activities include a Challenge. These extend your knowledge of Java by directing you to make changes in the Java source code.

Internet Support at Studio-JPlus

To further help you become proficient in Java, there is a Web site waiting for you. This site helps you get the most out of this book and your Java studies. The Web page directs you to some of the great Java Web pages in cyberspace. Since Java is so new, it is frequently being improved and updated. The Studio-JPlus Web site keeps you informed of these changes and improvements. Among the resources available to help you with your Java activities are:

• Sample Java applets
• Graphics
• Code samples
• Online Tests
• Study Guide
• Java news

One of the first proficiencies you will learn in Chapter 1 is how to find and use the Studio-JPlus Web site at:

http://www.studio-jplus.com

The Web page has many things to help you. First, there are examples of how the programs should look. Second, there are some classes that may not require you to enter in the Java source code by hand. Visit the Web site and copy the source code segments with the Copy command, then paste them to your Visual J++ software and complete your assignment. It is as easy as copy and paste! Also, the Java language is still very new. As a result, it often undergoes changes and revisions. Look to this Web site for updates.

Online Internet Study Guide and Testing for IDE Students

The *Java Activities Study Guide* can be found at the Studio-JPlus Web site. The Study Guide corresponds to the chapters and activities in this book. It is available to students using this book and can be downloaded over the Web from Studio-JPlus.

Use this guide as a reference to help you learn and remember all the detailed information that Java programmers and developers must know.

For Internet Distance Education (IDE) or independent study students, the Study Guide will help you prepare for the IDE tests. For more information about IDE support for this text, including quizzes, tests, and additional learning opportunities, see Activity 1.

The Internet Testing System found at Studio-JPlus provides tests and quizzes that will help you master the content of this book. The tests can be taken over the Internet using a Java applet created with the Visual J++ Developer Studio — the same Java development software you will use with this book.

Acknowledgments

Consulting Editor:
Minta Berry

Copy Editor:
Linda Allen – Good Guy Productions

Artwork:
Bill Heder – Internal Art
Terry Utley – Web site graphics

Java Rides the Web

Java is the programming language of the World Wide Web. JAVA allows **Web** users to run software programs directly from their Web browsers. **Browsers** that run Java include:

- **Internet Explorer** from **Microsoft** (3.0 or higher)
- **Netscape Navigator** from **Netscape Communications Corporation** (with Java plug-in)
- HotJavabrowser from **SUN Microsystems**

If you have a Java **applet**, you can place it on the Web and anyone with one of the Web browsers listed above can run the applet with a simple click of a mouse.

Java created a programming frenzy as millions of new applets have been created for the Web. Java is an essential programming language that allows all kinds of computers to take advantage of new and exciting Web-based software. Java and the Web will change the way we use and think about our computers. Java is a crucial component in the development of the next generation of cyber software.

Sector 1

In Chapter **1**   *On the Java Highway* will give you a look at how Java is being used on the Web today. The activities in this chapter will introduce you to applets on the Web and take you to the Studio-JPlus Web site.

In Chapter **2**   *On the Road to Object-Oriented Java Programming* traces the history of programming leading up to the object-oriented Java language. Java is a new language that is constantly changing and improving. You will learn how to stay up on all these changes in Activity 3.

On the Java Highway

Java was released to the Internet world in 1995. Java was created by Sun Microsystems as a compact programming language for programming electronic appliances, such as VCRs, satellite receivers, and microwaves. Little did the creators at Sun realize that Java would become the next big milestone in Internet software development.

First called "Greentalk" and later "Oak," Java was apparently named after a type of coffee several of the Sun developers were drinking the day they were asked to brainstorm a new name for their product. No one can explain how a cup of Java coffee relates to an Internet programming language. And, no one seems to remember the exact details of how the name came about, but it doesn't matter. As one Sun insider noted, "...we could have called it 'xyzzy' and it would still be popular."[1]

Why?

Java solves the problem of how to create software programs that can be delivered quickly and easily through the **World Wide Web**. Java will help change our computing lives. The editors of *Time* magazine understood the significance of Java when they named it one of the Ten Best Products of 1995.

Objectives:

- Discover what Java is and how it works on the Web.
- Surf the Web looking for Java applets and information pages.
- Review how to use a Web browser.
- Visit the Studio-JPlus Web site.
- View how Java <APPLET> HTML code looks on a Web page.
- Research the use of Java on the Web.
- Take a sample test and chapter test using a Java applet.

---

[1] Kieron Murphy, http://www.javaworld.com/javaworld/jw-10-1996/ jw-10-javaname.html, updated 15 September 1996.

What is Java?

Java is a programming language. It is used to create software.

Java specializes in creating small software programs called **applets**. These applets ride along Web pages all around the World Wide Web. When you create a Java applet, you are on the "leading edge" of software development on the expanding World Wide Web.

Java borrows some elements from the extremely popular **C++** programming language. C++ is responsible for most of the commercial software used today. Most of the software on your personal computer was created in C++.

Java eliminates many of the difficult concepts in C++ and gets right down to business. Java is more specialized than C++ and does some of its best work on the World Wide Web where it runs programs with the help of a Web browser. Java can also run stand-alone applications without the aid of a browser. This added dimension puts it a step ahead of many other programming languages and Web scripting languages like JavaScript, Perl, CGI, or VBScript.

In short, Java is a really cool programming language to learn.

If you are an experienced C++ programmer, learning Java should be relatively easy. If you have never learned a programming language before, Java is a great place to start because it is considered to be easier than C++ by many programmers and developers.

How Do Applets Work?

Java applets ride the Web like pizza rides inside a pizza delivery truck. When you call out for a pizza, the pizza is made, put into a box, loaded into the delivery truck, driven down the road, and delivered to your doorstep. You take delivery and enjoy. The pizza truck leaves and chomp, chomp, gulp, the pizza is gone. To get more pizza you must reorder.

Senore Appletto delivers virtual pizza on the superhighway

Java applets are like the pizza put safely inside a pizza box. Applets are placed inside HTML codes on Web pages. The World Wide Web is like the pizza delivery truck, which carries the pizza <APPLET> along the information superhighway to your doorstep. In this case, the Web delivers the <APPLET> to your personal computer.

FAQs

What is the difference between applications, applets, and executables?

Software developers use many terms to describe their software creations, including the terms *application*, *program*, *executable*, and now — *Web applet*. An applet is any software program that can run on the World Wide Web with the help of a Web browser. A Java application is a software program that runs on a computer without the help of a Java-enabled browser. An executable is any software program that runs on a computer. Both applets and applications are executable software programs. Executables are easy to spot in Windows because they usually have a **.exe** extension in their name. Look for ".exe's" on your hard drive!

Why put angle brackets around the word <APPLET>?

Web pages can carry an <APPLET> across the Web to anyone who wants or needs to use it. Then, with the help of a Java-enabled Web browser — chomp, chomp, gulp — the program runs and does what the Java programmer intended. When you surf to a new Web page, the <APPLET> goes away as the new Web page appears.

What Does a Java <APPLET> Tag Look Like?

The best way to understand Java is to order an <APPLET> from the World Wide Web. In Activity 1, you will surf the Web to several key Java sites and experience Java firsthand. Here is what you are looking for:

n HTML, angle brackets < > denote a command or instruction to a Web browser. Words in brackets are called <TAGS>. The specific tag that tells the browser to run a Java applet is <APPLET>. We put brackets around <APPLET> in this section so you would wonder what in the world we were doing and investigate this Frequently Asked Question.

• Objects that move
• Pictures that are constantly changing
• Sounds
• Animation
• Video clips
• Interactive games
• Useful charts and statistics that are constantly updated
• Software programs that do almost anything!

You will find Web applets on Web pages. The Web pages are created using another language called HTML. **HTML** is short for <u>H</u>yper<u>T</u>ext <u>M</u>arkup Language. HTML uses special tags that tell a Web browser how to display a document. Figure 1.1 shows HTML tags. Everything enclosed in angle brackets is an **HTML tag**.

HTML allows for <APPLET> tags to be placed inside HTML Web pages. The relationship between HTML and Java <APPLETS> is similar to pizza in a pizza box. HTML is the box; the Java <APPLET> is the pizza inside. HTML allows the <APPLET> to be transported in a nice, neat, protected little package until it can be displayed to the end user. With a click and double-click, the HTML box is opened and the <APPLET> goes into action.

You can see <APPLET> tags on HTML Web pages by clicking on the **View**, **Source** command on your Web browser. (See Figure 1.2.)

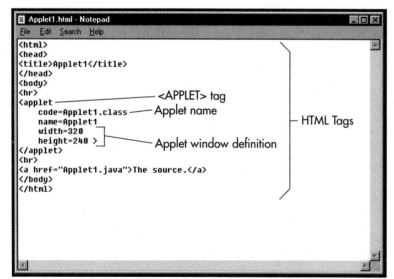

```
Applet1.html - Notepad
File  Edit  Search  Help
<html>
<head>
<title>Applet1</title>
</head>
<body>
<hr>
<applet ─────────────── <APPLET> tag
    code=Applet1.class ── Applet name
    name=Applet1
    width=320
    height=240 > ─────── Applet window definition
</applet>
<hr>
<a href="Applet1.java">The source.</a>
</body>
</html>
                                          ├─ HTML Tags
```

Figure 1.1
HTML tags

HTML box,
<APPLET> Pizza

Senore Appletto displaying
Pizza in a box

In Activity 1, you will visit several Web pages and view the HTML source documents to see how Java applets are embedded into Web pages.

Hint! Look for the angle brackets around the word <APPLET>.

Applets are Portable

Java applets are portable. **Portability** refers to the ability of Java applets to run or work on any computer **platform**, including these different kinds of computers:

- Windows
- Unix
- Macintosh

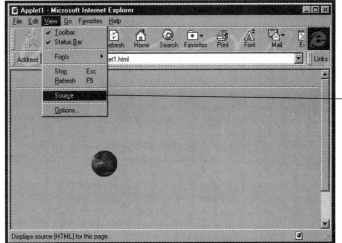

HTML Source Tags

Figure 1.2
View Source Command

In other words, when you write a program in Java and put it on the Web, any computer can load and run your applet if they have a Java-enabled browser. The applet can "port" or transfer itself to any computer and still do what the **programmer** or **developer** of the applet intended.

Java-enabled browsers include:

- Internet Explorer from Microsoft
- Netscape Navigator from Netscape Communications Corporation
- HotJava Browser from SUN Microsystems

Each of these browsers has a Java **interpreter** inside. The Java interpreter is the key to Java's portability. When the Java applet is selected from a Web page, the Java interpreter is activated. The interpreter converts the Java <APPLET> codes into the specific computer language your personal computer understands.

Running JAVA <APPLETS> on the Web

There are several steps in delivering a Java applet on the World Wide Web (WWW) so it can run inside a browser:

1. **Create** a Java applet with Visual J++.
2. **Post** or place the applet on a Web server with the help of your Webmaster. (The applet will need to be embedded inside an HTML page.)

FAQs

What is the difference between a Java programmer and a Java developer?

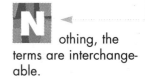

othing, the terms are interchangeable.

3. **Load** the applet into your Java-enabled browser by keying the Web page address on the WWW.

4. Your Java-enabled browser will **interpret** the applet's Java code.

5. **Run** or start the Java applet. Most applets begin to run as soon as the HTML Web page loads into your browser.

To help you find your way around the superhighway, we have created a Web site called Studio-JPlus at:

http://www.studio-jplus.com/

This Web site will help you see applets from all over the WWW. In fact, if you have your Java-enabled browser currently loaded on your personal computer, you can run Web applets. As the WWW changes, the Studio-JPlus Web site will be updated to reflect the changes. So if the locations or applets described in this book should ever become obsolete, you can access new ones by visiting Studio-JPlus.

In Activity 1, you will visit several Java sites. Some have applets to run; others have information about Java. You are now on the Java Superhighway! So, bring along a few pizzas; you may not want to end your trip for awhile!

Debriefing

The pizza truck analogy helps explain how Java and the World Wide Web (WWW) work together:

- The pizza delivery truck is like information traveling on the WWW. You can summon Java applets to be delivered to your browser window, just like you can have pizza delivered to your home.
- Think of applets as pizzas. When you open the box (or double-click the applet with your mouse), you get the pizza you asked for, complete with toppings. In this example the HTML Web page is the box, and the <APPLET> is inside the box waiting to be opened. When you open the box, zing, you have a Java applet running on your computer!
- Think of the pizza maker as a programmer, the person who creates the applet.
- Once the pizza has been delivered, the pizza truck drives away, just like a Web page disappears when you are finished with it.

Applets allow programmers and developers to create programs and post their executables on a Web page for display and execution by the requesting computer. With Java, you can create application programs and make them part of a Web page. These Java applets can execute inside a Java-enabled Web browser. After the applet is finished executing, it returns to the Web page and disappears. Figure 1.2 shows a sample of an HTML <APPLET> tag.

Take a Test!

In Activity 1, you will learn how to take a test using a Java applet over the World Wide Web. The Java test engine called the Internet Testing System was created using Visual J++ from Microsoft. (See Figure 1.3.)

List of Terms

To help you prepare to take your first Java online test, review this list of terms. Can you define each one?

Applets
Browser
C++
Developer
HTML
HTML tag
Internet Explorer
Interpreter
Java
Java-enabled browsers
Microsoft
Netscape Navigator
Platform
Portability
Post
Programmer
SUN Microsystems
Web
World Wide Web (WWW)

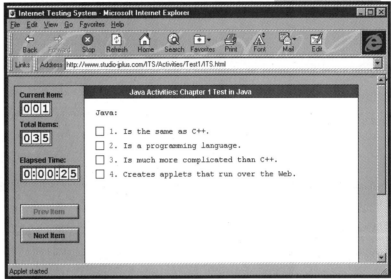

Students of this book can take a test on the Web with any Java-enabled browser on any type of computer.

Figure 1.3
The Internet Testing System is a Java applet that rides the Web.

Delivering Java Anywhere, Anytime

Businesses are delivering Java applets to their customers wherever and whenever they need them over the World Wide Web (WWW). By visiting these sites, you can see how Java is being used in the virtual world of the Web. You will be able to get ideas about what you can do with Java.

The activities in Sector 1 do not require you to know how to program in Java. There is no special software to run. All you need is a Java-enabled Web browser like Microsoft's Internet Explorer. With a Java-enabled browser, you can experience Java at any time from any Web connection on the globe.

In this activity, you will review the important Web browser skills you need as you visit the Java resources on the Web and the information at Studio-JPlus.

O b j e c t i v e s :

- Start your Web browser.
- Enter the URL for the Studio-JPlus home page.
- Bookmark the Studio-JPlus Study Guide home page.
- Visit several Java sites.
- Recognize the Java HTML <APPLET> tags.
- Search for new Java and Visual J++ resources on the Web.
- Observe and record how Java is used on the Web.
- Take a sample test using a Java test engine created with Visual J++.
- Exit your browser.

Step 1: Start your Web browser by double-clicking on the browser icon as shown in Figure A1.1.

Figure A1.1
The Internet Explorer
Browser Icon

The Internet

Step 2: To enter the URL for the Studio-JPlus Web page:

2A: Click the **File** menu.

2B: Select **Open** (or **Open Location** in Netscape) as shown in Figure A1.2.

Activity 1 Searching for Java

Figure A1.2
The File Menu
A – Click File,
B – Select Open

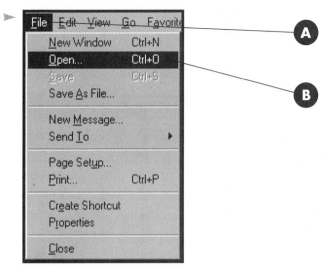

2C: Enter the URL for the Studio-JPlus Web Page exactly as follows:

http://www.studio-jplus.com/

2D: Did you find Studio-JPlus? Now try another URL. This address will take you to the specific Web page for this book. It is similar, but you add the filename **appletto.html**. Enter it exactly as shown below.

http://www.studio-jplus.com/appletto.html

Figure A1.3
Enter the Studio-JPlus
Web page URL
C – Enter URL for the
Appletto.html Web page
on Studio-JPlus

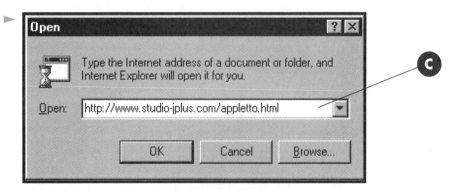

Debug: A word of caution — you should enter the URL exactly as shown. If one letter is incorrect, or if you add any spaces, you will not end up where you want to be!

Step 3: To add the Studio-JPlus Web page to your favorites list, click the **Favorites** menu and select **Add to Favorites** in Internet Explorer. (Select **Bookmarks** and **Add Bookmark** in Netscape.)

Figure A1.4
The Studio-JPlus Home
Page
A – Click Add to
Favorites
B – Activity 1 link
C – Chapter 1 Test link

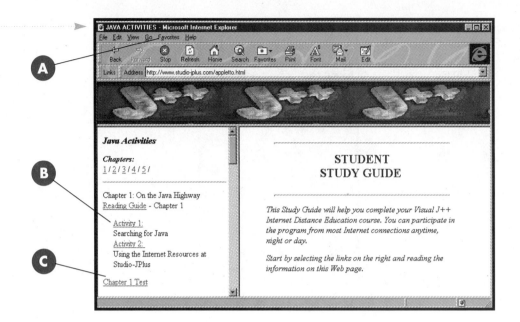

Debug: Click your **Favorites** (or **Bookmarks**) menu and make sure you can see Studio-JPlus in your favorites list. Visit several Web pages, then try your Studio-JPlus favorites link by clicking on it.

//Comment: Now that you have bookmarked or added the Studio-JPlus Web site to your favorites list, you can return to it as often as you like by clicking on the item in the list.

Step 4: To use the Studio-JPlus Web site:

4A: Use the scroll bar to move up and down the Studio-JPlus Web page.

4B: Scroll until you see the hypertext link for Activity 1. Click on the link.

4C: In Activity 1, you will see a list of suggested sites to visit. Try each link by clicking on the underlined words. When you make a selection, you will be taken to the requested Web page. After you have viewed it, return to this page by using the **Back** button or by clicking the Studio-JPlus favorites item from the **Favorites** or **Bookmarks** menu.

4D: Use the **Back** and **Forward** buttons to move back and forward between the various Web pages you have found. Use the **Home** button to return to your starting Web page.

//Comment: The sites in the list are well-known Java sites. Can you find any more? Add your favorite sites to your Favorites or Bookmarks list.

Debriefing

This activity involved practicing many essential Web browser proficiencies that are necessary to get the most out of this course. The Studio-JPlus Web site will help you in your pursuit of Java. One of the valuable resources on Studio JPlus is the online Internet Testing System. These tests are delivered over the Web by a Java applet! Try a test and see what Java can be like.

Take a Test!

Tutorial tests can be taken over the Internet. They are found on the Studio-JPlus Web site. These tests will help you understand the terms, concepts, and ideas found in the text.

To demonstrate you have mastered the objectives in this activity, perform the steps described below. The steps will lead you to the Chapter 1 tutorial online test on the Studio-JPlus Web site. Take the Chapter 1 tutorial test to see what you have learned.

Remember, the Internet Testing System that delivers the chapter tutorial tests is a real Java applet created with Visual J++, the same software you will begin using in Chapter 2.

Are you ready to show what you know? Then begin!

1. Open your browser.
2. Use your Favorites list to return to the Studio-JPlus Web site (http://www.studio-jplus.com/appletto.html).
3. Scroll down and find the hypertext link *Chapter 1 Test*, as marked in Figure A1.4.
4. Read the information on the home page.
5. Add this page to your Favorites list.
6. Click on the *Chapter 1 Test*. Answer all the questions. (How did you do? Don't worry if you didn't do well, you can take these tests as often as you like!)
7. Click on the **Summary** button and get a summary of your sample test.
8. Click back to your Score Report page and click on the **Submit** button.
9. Follow the instructions to submit your test results to your instructor, parent, or to yourself via e-mail.
10. Return to your Score Report page and exit the Visual J++ Internet Testing System applet by clicking the **Back** button or by entering another URL.

//Comment: If you don't like your score, open your book, review your answers, and try again. There is no penalty for doing these tests over and over again.

hy be in the dark?

Why be in the dark about what is expected in this course? There is help on the Web. There are people to contact, Java sites to visit, and help in cyberspace.

Many schools don't teach Java, so a great number of students are learning Java with the help of the Internet in a program called **Internet Distance Education,** or IDE for short. The Studio-JPlus Web site provides many of the resources needed to learn with the help of the Internet.

About The Studio-JPlus IDE Learning Resources

A brief description of the various Studio-JPlus IDE resources follows:

- The **Reading Guide** outlines what you need to know and remember out of each chapter in the text. The reading guide will be a very valuable resource while you study your text.
- **Activity Links** provide online support and information that can help you with what you are trying to accomplish.
- The **Chapter Test** link allows you to take your practice (tutorial) tests over the Web. The Internet Testing System is an actual Java applet that will allow you to take a test, view a scoring report, and submit the results to your instructor or parent.
- The online **Glossary** defines the words that Java programmers use.
- **MainFunction** is an online resource for programming students. MainFunction has many resources to help C++, Visual Basic, and Java students.

In this activity, you will return to the Studio-JPlus Web site and learn to use the online Java Activities IDE learning resources.

O b j e c t i v e s :

- Locate and use the Java Activities support pages and applets at Studio-Jplus.
- Read the IDE Study Guide.
- Visit the Activity links for Activities 1 and 2.
- Take your Chapter 1 Test.
- Use online Java Activities Glossary.
- Visit MainFunction.

Step 1: Start your Web browser.

Step 2: Locate the Studio-JPlus Java Activities Web page from   r bookmark or favorites list or enter the following URL as explained i.   :tivity 1, Step 2:

http://www.studio-jplus.com/appletto.html

Note: If you did not add Studio-JPlus or the appletto.html Web page to your favorites or bookmarks list, or if you need help finding Studio-JPlus, review Activity 1.

Activity 2 · Using the Internet Resources at Studio-JPlus

//Comment: Use the hypertext links to move through the IDE support materials as marked in Figure A2.1.

Figure A2.1
The appletto.html Web Page
A – Select the chapter you want to visit
B – Click the Reading Guide
C – Click the Activity links
D – Choose the Chapter Test link

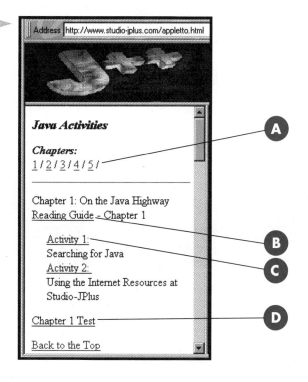

Step 3: To explore the Java Activities Web page at Studio-JPlus:

3A: Click on the *Chapter* link you need to visit as marked in Figure A2.1.

3B: Click on the *Reading Guide* link. Use the scroll bar to move up and down the reading guide.
Hint! Return using the Back button.

3C: Click any of the *Activity* links to view the options that are provided. Be certain to click the *Activity 2* link! What did you find there?
Note: You can view, copy, and paste source code from this Web site for many of the more difficult programming activities appearing later in this book.

3D: Try various links. What did you find? Did you learn anything new about Java?

Reading Guide

The reading guide will help you prepare for the online tests. If an item is not listed in the reading guide, it will not appear on the chapter's tutorial test. You can print the reading guide chapter by chapter, or you can copy the contents of the chapter's reading guide to your word processor and answer the questions in an electronic file.

Step 4: To print a copy of a chapter's reading guide:

4A: Click on the _Reading Guide_ link for Chapter 1 marked in Figure A2.1.

4B: Click on the **File** menu and select **Print**.

Step 5: To copy and paste the Chapter 1 reading guide from the Web site to your word processor:

5A: Click on the Chapter 1 link as marked in Figure A2.1.

5B: When the Chapter 1 reading guide appears, choose **Select All** from the **Edit** menu as shown in Figure A2.2.

Figure A2.2
Chapter 1 Reading Guide
B – Click Select All
C – Click Copy

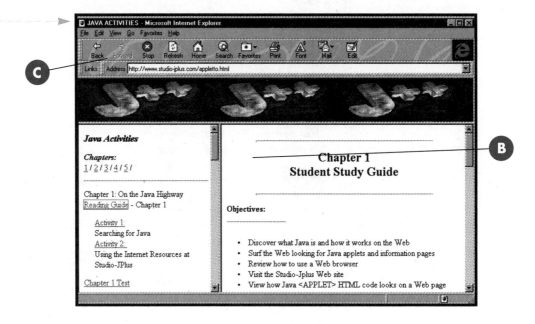

5C: Select **Copy** from the **Edit** menu.

5D: Open your word processor.

5E: Select **Paste** from the **Edit** menu and the text will appear.

 //Comment: You can now answer the reading guide questions in your word processor and save a copy on your computer for later study. If you need to e-mail your work to your instructor, you can use the attach feature on your e-mail system, or copy and paste your answers to your e-mail message window.

Internet Testing System

Tutorial tests are given at the end of each chapter. These tests are designed to help you learn by focusing your attention on items in the book that are important.

Step 6: To take the Chapter 1 test over the Internet:

6A: Click on the *Chapter 1 Test* link marked in Figure A2.1.

6B: Read the instructions given about how to take a test. Use the scroll bar to read the entire document.

6C: Click on the *Chapter 1 Tutorial Test* link. Your test should load just like a regular HTML Web page.

 Debug: If your test does not appear, several things may be wrong:

1. You may not have a Java-enabled Web browser.
   Solution: Install the latest version of Internet Explorer.

2. One of the many servers, computers, or routers in the path between you and the testing center may be down.
   Solution: Try again later.

3. There may be a problem with that particular test.
   Solution: Use the **Refresh** or **Reload** command and try again.

6D: Answer the questions as directed. Did you do better this time?

 //Comment: When the questions display circles, only one answer is needed. When squares appear in the questions then more than one answer is required.

6E: When the test is over, click the **Summary** button to see how you did on individual items. You will be instructed on how to review missed items.

 //Comment: If you don't like your score, go back and study with the help of your reading guide. Take the test again when you feel ready.

6F: Click the **Submit** button if you want your results to be shared with your instructor, parent, or if you want to e-mail a copy of the results to yourself.

6G: Click the Back button to return to the menu, or enter another URL to go to another Web site.

Glossary

The Glossary provides definitions for words used in Java and the computer programming industry.

Step 7: To view the Glossary:

7A: Scroll down until you see the *Glossary* link on the Java Activities Web page. Click on the *Glossary* link.

7B: Click on the letter **M**.

7C: Scroll down and read the definition for "method."

7D: Scroll to the bottom of the Glossary. What is the last word in the glossary?

MainFunction

MainFunction is a Web site devoted to programming students and programming topics. This is a place where Java, C++, and Visual Basic students can meet to share ideas and information. (See Figure A2.3.) There are articles and lots of things going on at MainFunction.

Step 8: To visit MainFunction:

8A: Click the **MainFunction** button on the Java Activities Web page on Studio-JPlus, or enter the following URL:

> *http://www.mainfunction.com/*

8B: Return to the Studio-JPlus site by clicking the Back button.

Figure A2.3
www.MainFunction.com

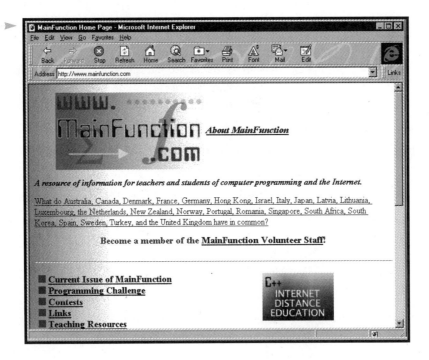

Debriefing

The Internet Distance Education resources you have just visited on the Web have one major goal — to help you study and successfully learn Java.

Okay, tests can be a bit scary, even if they are given over the Internet by a friendly Java applet. Relax! You can repeat the tutorial tests. After taking the Chapter 1 tutorial test, you will see any topics you may need to restudy. When you feel doubly prepared, retake the Chapter 1 tutorial test. When you view tests as learning tools, you won't be too nervous about test taking.

Don't forget to use the Glossary and Reading Guide to help you review any words or concepts you don't know or don't understand.

Chapter 2

On the Road to Object-Oriented Java Programming

The road to Java has been paved by other programming languages. Dating back 30 years, machine, assembly, and other languages were used to program computers. These low-level languages spoke to the very insides of a computer where only zeros and ones are spoken.

Eventually higher level languages made talking to a computer easier. This chapter traces the evolution of programming languages up to Java.

One thing you learn quickly about a programming language as dynamic as Java is that you can't learn it all from books. Books are great, but how many times have you gone to your favorite book or encyclopedia and found the information out of date or obsolete? It's the same with the fast-moving world of Java programming.

Cyberspace may not be the best place to learn some things, like shooting a basketball or playing the trombone, but *it certainly is the best place to learn about rapidly changing technical topics like Java and Visual J++.*

There are many ways people share information on the Net, including Web pages, listserves, e-mail, newsgroups, or chat groups. Java programmers quickly learn that staying current means being online and tuned into the Internet. In Activity 3, you will learn to find the sources of Java information used by many professionals.

Objectives:

- Review how Java is used on the Web.
- Discover how the binary numbering system is used to communicate to computer processors.
- Compare Java to other programming languages.
- Learn why Java is an excellent programming language for the Web.
- Understand object-oriented programming.
- Define classes.
- View how classes are used to build a Java applet.
- Tune into what the professionals are saying about Java.
- Find new Java learning resources on the Internet.

The Many Uses of Java

In Activities 1 and 2, you were able to see for yourself how Java is being used on the World Wide Web. If you tried all the links in the activities, you saw how Java is used to:

- Create moving objects (animation)
- Program interactive computer games
- Develop useful applications people can use over the Web
- Present constantly changing data and information
- Test your knowledge of Java

People use the Internet and World Wide Web for communication, entertainment, and for work. The Net has become an important new part of our lives. If your Net connection is properly wired, you can listen to radio stations from around the world or watch your favorite television program in a corner of your computer screen. At the same time, you can write and submit a report for school, e-mail your friends and instructors, or post your work as a home page. You can look up almost anything with the help of a search engine, and move information you find on the Web to your personal hard drive. All this interactivity requires programming.

Everything we see in cyberspace was created, directly or indirectly, by programmers. Programmers use programming languages to accomplish electronic "cyber magic." Java is a programming language ideally suited for use on the Internet. Java applet programs must talk to every kind of computer used on the Net.

How to Talk to Computers

When most of us think of computers, we think of boxes with a monitor and a keyboard attached. However, other types of computers are very common. In fact, computers can be found everywhere. You will find them inside wristwatches, household appliances, and behind the clock that blinks 12:00 on your VCR. Most cars have several computers under the hood. Airport and mall security surveillance systems are run by miniature computers. Some toasters and microwaves even have computers in them. Java was created specifically to program instructions for these specialized computers.

Computers aren't easy to talk to — because computers aren't very smart! Computers only understand numbers, not words. What's more, computers can't even count to 2. It takes programmers to make computers look intelligent.

Believe it or not, computers can only count from zero to one. Yet, we use computers to calculate much higher numbers — into the millions of billions.

How is it possible for a machine that can't count past one to process numbers that high? Three things help to make it possible:

- Circuits
- The power of two numbers
- The speed of electricity

Circuits

The part of the computer that "thinks" is called the central processing unit (CPU). The CPU consists of millions and millions of miniaturized **circuits**. These circuits are like on/off switches, similar to the on and off switches on your computer, your television, and your CD player. Each of these millions of circuits can either be off (represented by 0) or on (represented by 1).

The Power of Two Numbers

How can two numbers, 0 and 1, be used to count? A numbering system called binary makes it possible for you to count as high as you want on a computer. The first part of the word binary (bi) means two. Therefore, the **binary numbering system** uses only two numbers, 0 and 1. For most of us, counting in binary seems a little strange.

It is easier to see how binary works if we compare it to the decimal system most people use every day. The **decimal system** is based on 10. (For humans, a numbering system based on the number of fingers and thumbs on two hands is an easy system to remember.)

How do you translate decimal number into binary numbers? We will use the decimal number 15 as an example. In binary, 15 is the number 1111. To demonstrate, compare decimal to binary:

Binary		Decimal
0	=	0
1	=	1
10	=	2
11	=	3
100	=	4
101	=	5
110	=	6
111	=	7
1000	=	8
1001	=	9
1010	=	10
1011	=	11
1100	=	12
1101	=	13
1110	=	14
1111	=	15

Can you see the pattern? Binary works just like the decimal system. In the decimal you have ten numbers to work with — 0 to 9. When counting to fifteen in decimal, you start by counting 0, 1, 2, 3, 4, 5, 6, 7, 8, 9. When you get to the number 9 you run out of numbers and automatically move a 1 into a place called the tens place and keep adding ones in the ones place to equal 15.

Ten's place

1 ten and 5 ones = 15

One's place

If you need to count to 115, you add a hundreds place. For 1,115 you add a thousands place and so on until you count as high as you want to go. For example:

Thousand's place

Ten's place

1 thousand, 1 hundred, 1 ten and 5 ones = 1,115

One's place

Hundred's place

Binary works the same way. When counting to fifteen in binary, you start by counting 0, 1. When you get to the number 1, you run out of numbers and automatically move to the two's place and keep adding.

0	=	0
1	=	1
10	=	2
11	=	3

When you get to the binary number 11, you must create a four's place in order to continue. A four's place allows you to count to the binary number 7 before you run out of digits.

100	=	4
101	=	5
110	=	6
111	=	7

Notice that each time we add a place in the binary system it is a multiple of 2. In other words, 1*2=2, 2*2=4, 2*4=8, 2*8=16, 2*16=32. This is called the power of 2. The power of 2 is essential to understanding computers.

To continue counting, you must add a place for the number 8. With the eight's place, you can count to 15 in binary.

1000	=	8
1001	=	9
1010	=	10
1011	=	11
1100	=	12
1101	=	13
1110	=	14
1111	=	15

The Speed of Electricity

Computers using only 0's and 1's can count very, very fast. How fast? As fast as electricity can travel through the circuits of the computer processor. At this speed, millions of calculations can now be made in seconds. Imagine, millions of circuits turning on and off each second inside of your computer's CPU.

Don't worry if you can't speak binary. Your computer will understand it. Besides, programming languages were created so that you don't have to speak binary. Programming languages like Java represent a more natural way for people, who use words, to communicate with computers and machines.

For now, simply remember that computers think in binary numbers and process information quickly by manipulating millions and millions of binary circuits at the speed of electricity.

A Quick History of Programming Languages before Java

Programmers use a variety of programming languages to give instructions to computers. The most common types of programming languages include:

• Machine language
• Assembly language
• Procedural languages
• Object-oriented programming languages

Knowing just a little about how a computer is programmed and how these other languages work will help you appreciate the advantages of using Java.

Machine Language

If computers only speak in binary digits, in other words, in 0's and 1's, then how do programmers talk to computers? The answer is, in binary. It is the only language a computer's processor understands.

One of the first ways programmers communicated with computers was with machine language. Machine language commands look like binary numbers. For example:

01010101
100001011 11101100
01001100
01001100

This primitive machine communication is a language a machine can relate to! However, it only takes one look at machine language to understand why programming languages were invented. Let's face it, it is very hard for humans to remember all of these numbers and exactly what each number does.

Assembly Language

To avoid having to program a computer with binary commands, programmers invented computer programming languages. One of the first programming languages was called "**Assembly**." Assembly is a lower level language, meaning Assembly is more like machine language than most of the popular programming languages used today.

Assembly language uses words or assembly commands that are then turned into machine specific commands. Here is a sample of Assembly language:

PUSH BP
MOV BP,SP
DEC SP
DEC SP

There are some advantages to low-level languages, including increased processing speed and low memory requirements. However, the disadvantages of Assembly are obvious. Assembly, like binary and machine language, is still hard to remember. So, higher level languages were created. The first **high-level languages** were called procedural programming languages.

Procedural Languages

The first **procedural languages** included such legendary programming languages as Basic, Fortran, and Cobol. Early versions of C and Pascal were also procedural languages. Procedural languages allowed the programmer to think about what procedures or functions the software was to perform.

Procedural languages focus the attention of the programmer on the actual processes the software is going to perform, rather than worrying about the specific machine level commands the computer needs to know. Software tools called **compilers** converted the procedures into machine specific commands.

FAQs

What is the difference between a low-level and a high-level language?

Each computer processor has a set of instructions it understands. This set of instructions is cleverly named "the instructional set." **Low-level languages** speak directly to this instructional set with binary numbers or codes. Higher level languages, like Basic, Pascal, C++, and Java worry more about what the programmer wants to accomplish and then translates, or compiles, the programmer's ideas into lower machine level instructions. Lower level languages include machine and assembly languages. The other languages discussed in this book are higher level languages.

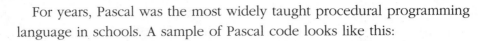

For years, Pascal was the most widely taught procedural programming language in schools. A sample of Pascal code looks like this:

```
program AddIt;
var
      i, j, k : integer;
 begin
      i := 3;
      j := 2;
      k := i + j;
 end.
```

Pascal still looks pretty strange to non-programmers, but at least the programmer didn't have to remember all the binary 1's and 0's or the assembly commands. (Some of the words in Pascal like *begin, end, program,* and *integer* are even readable!) Procedural languages created most of the software for computers in the 1980s and early 1990s. Procedural languages were a big step forward in the improvement of the programming process.

Object-Oriented Programming Languages

Procedural languages still require a lot of work. Every operation, procedure, or function must be programmed a line at a time — and that requires a lot of keyboarding! Programmers began to search for a better, even faster way to program. So, object-oriented programming was invented. (Object-oriented programming is explained in more detail in the next section of this chapter.)

One of the first widely known object-oriented programming languages was C++. C++ was built upon a procedural language called C. C++ is responsible for most of the software used on microcomputers today. C++ is a very powerful language, perhaps too powerful.

C++ added a bunch of "extra stuff" to C, in some users' opinions cluttering it up. C++ is a language that tries to do everything possible. Therefore, many things about C++ could be simplified. In other words, there are some things about C++ that sometimes can seem unnecessarily complex.

Java benefits from C++'s growing pains. Many of the complexities of C++ have simply been left out of Java. Java was created from scratch as a true object-oriented programming language. Java borrowed the best ideas from C++ and the best ideas from other object-oriented programming languages, and started over. Former C++ programmers using Java for the first time report that there are many things they simply don't have to worry about anymore, leaving them free to work on their applets.

Finding a Suitable Computer Language for the Internet

The Internet created a series of problems for which C++ and other object-oriented languages are not well suited. Java is very suitable for the Net because it is a programming language that:

1. Is object-oriented.

2. Works on many different kinds of computers (i.e., Macintosh, IBMs, IBM clones, SUN workstations, UNIX workstations, etc.).

3. Works reliably with the many different computer operating systems in use (i.e., MacOS, UNIX, OS2, Windows, NEXT, SUN OS).

4. Protects computers from viruses that can be passed from computer to computer very easily on the Net.

5. Produces small, "fast" code that can travel over the Net via slow modems.

6. Provides security and protection from computer hackers.

Other languages, like C++, can't do all of these six items well. Java takes the next step, providing a solution for the future of Internet computer programming.

And then, OOPs, it was Java!

When it comes to Internet software development, Java runs OOPs around other programming languages. **OOP** is short for object-oriented programming. You can say O, O, P, or you can say "OOP" as in "OOPs, I slopped pizza all over my new shirt!"

To understand OOP you need only understand how pizza is made.

Senore Appletto makes his pizza dough by hand. He spreads his special sauce with eleven herbs and spices over the dough. Then, he adds his carefully selected toppings: cheese, pepperoni, olives, mushrooms, and special diced green chilies for extra flavor.

Each element of the pizza is an object. Some objects Appletto makes by hand; others he buys at the local market. To create an entire pizza requires many ingredients. Each ingredient exists without the pizza, but no single ingredient can be called pizza! Only when the ingredients are combined in a certain way can it be called the "Pizza Deluxe."

It is the same with Java applets. Ingredients are called **classes** in Java-speak. In java-pizza terms, you have:

• A dough or bread class
• A sauce class
• A cheese class

Many early computer programming languages like Basic, Pascal, and C weren't object oriented. They were procedural languages, requiring the programmer to sequence every little command or function and to create entire programs from the ground up. This meant lots of extra work. As you will see in the sections that follow, OOP languages like Java allow classes or "objects" to be used over and over again in many different programs, saving the programmer lots of programming time.

- A meat and cholesterol class
- A veggie class including such things as olives, mushrooms, and hot chiles

When you combine these classes of ingredients, you get something new, something different — namely:

- A pizza class!

OOP is like creating different kinds of pizza. Think of each element of the pizza as an object. Combining objects creates new objects. These objects can be changed again and again to create new and even better objects, just like the toppings can be changed to create a new kind of pizza. In scientific terms this could be called object-oriented pizza making. (You can tell that OOP is about as far away from binary machine language programming as you can get! Forget about the 0's and 1's; bring on the pizza!)

From Pizza to Applet

Let's compare the pizza example with some real Java software. You don't have to look very far to see how pizza and applets are alike.

The Internet Testing System you have been using to take your tests is made up of ingredients or objects called classes. Using the steps you learned in Activity 2, hit the Web and open the sample tutorial test. Find the status bar in Figure 2.1.

Start your Internet Testing System and start the sample tutorial test. (See Activity 2 if you need help.) As your testing applet begins to load, watch the status bar carefully. You will see the classes or Java ingredients loading one by one. Don't blink or you will miss one! They include the:

- ITS.class
- ITSCounter.class
- ITSItem.class
- ITSTimer.class
- ITSButton.class
- ITSTest.class
- ITSAlt.class
- ITSGroup.class

It's time to play a matching game. Can you match three or four of the class names listed above with the picture in Figure 2.1?

Check your answers by comparing them to Figure 2.2. The answers are marked there. How did you do?

Learn More about Java on the Web

As you can tell from the history lesson about the progression of computer programming languages from machine language to Java, programming languages are constantly evolving. It is likely that computer programming languages will continue to develop as new ways are found to improve our communications with computers. OOP may soon become obsolete.

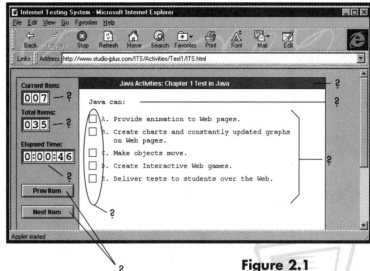

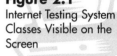

As you will see in Activity 6, Java Applet Wizards can create much of your program for you automatically. Rapid-application development tools make programming a software application even faster.

Figure 2.1
Internet Testing System Classes Visible on the Screen

To keep track of these constant improvements, a programmer must use the Internet to learn about important changes in the field of programming. In Activity 3, you will search for sites that will help you learn even more about Java and other programming solutions.

Debriefing

Java is a language perfectly suited for small, compact little programs, like those that run on small appliances, microwaves, and watches. These attributes also make it a good programming language for the Internet where small, fast programs must be used.

Java also has certain other advantages and security features built into it that make it Internet friendly. In Activity 3, see if you can discover additional advantages of Java from information on the Net.

Take a Test!
Time to take a test and see how much you remember from this chapter. Log into the Internet Testing System and get an A+.

1. Enter the following URL or Internet address:

http://www.studio-jplus.com/appletto.html

2. Select Chapter 2.
3. Click the *Chapter 2 Test* link.

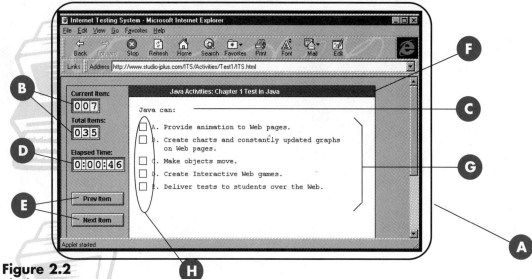

Figure 2.2
Check Your Answers
A - ITS.class,
B - ITSCounter.class,
C - ITSItem.class,
D - ITSTimer.class,
E - ITSButton.class,
F - ITSTest.class,
G - ITSSAlt.class,
H - ITSGroup.class

4.   Take the test. How did you do?

5.   When you have finished, exit the testing system and close your browser.

Proficiency Test 2

Count in binary from 0 to 65. (Hint: 16 = 10000)

List of Terms

Assembly language
Binary numbering system
Circuits
Classes
Compilers
Decimal system
High-level languages
Low-level languages
Machine language
Object-oriented programming (OOP)
Procedural programming languages

oing Beyond the Book

You can't learn everything you need to know about Java from this, or any other, book. There is always more to learn. Fortunately, the Web can help. There are plenty of places you can go to expand your understanding about Java, how it works, and how it is used. Search engines are a good place to begin. Search engines allow you to search topics of interest on the Net. There are also newsgroups and listserves dedicated to Java. Finding and using these resources will add to your Java experience.

O   b   j   e   c   t   i   v   e   s   :

- Start your Web browser.
- Enter the URL for the Studio-JPlus home page.
- Find various search engines.
- Search various Java related topics on the Web.
- Locate newsgroups that discuss Java.
- Investigate listserves that discuss Java.
- Take a sample test using a Java test engine created with Visual J++.
- Exit your browser.

Step 1:   Start your Web browser.

Step 2:   Select the Java Activities Studio-JPlus link from your favorites or bookmarks list.

 //Comment: Enter the URL for the Studio-JPlus Web page:

http://www.studio-jplus.com/appletto.html

Step 3:   Select the *Activity 3* link or click on the **Search Engines** button. Select any search engine from the list.

 //Comment: You can also find search engines quickly by clicking the appropriate button on your browser.

Activity 3 Finding Java Resources in Cyberspace

Step 4: When any of the search engine windows appear, enter the following terms and do a search.

- Java
- Visual J++
- Java Applets
- HTML
- Internet Explorer
- Netscape Navigator
- HotJava
- SUN Microsystems
- Microsoft

 //Comment: What resources did you find? Use your bookmark or favorites list to keep track of the important sites. You can also select **File**, **Print** to print copies of important Web pages.

 Debug: If a page comes into your browser unnaturally slow, click the **Stop** button, then select **Refresh** or **Reload**. Often it is better to stop a page and ask for a new copy than it is to wait, and wait, and wait.

FAQs

What is a search engine?

he term *search engine* applies to a growing set of tools that search the Internet for information on various topics. Your browser will allow you to find and use search engines. Some of our favorites search engines include:

http://lycos.cs.cmu.edu/
Lycos Search Engine

http://home.mcom.com/
home/internet-search.html
Netscape Search Engine

http://webcrawler.com/
WebCrawler

http://web.nexor.co.uk/
public/aliweb/search/
doc/form.html
ALIWEB Search

http://
www.dejanews.com/
Deja News Research

http://www.excite.com
Excite

http://www.mckinley.com
Magellean

http://altavista.digital.com/
AltaVista by Digital Corp

http://
hoohoo.ncsa.uiuc.edu/
archie.html
Archie

Review the top five sites you have found and complete the following table.

#	URL or Web Address	List the Title of the Web Page	Give a brief description of the Java-related Web site
Sample	http://www.studio-jplus.com/student.html	The Studio-JPlus Web site	Contains information to help students using the textbook *Java Activities*.
1			
2			
3			
4			
5			

Debriefing

This activity asked you to go beyond the book and to find new sources that can help you extend your knowledge of Java and Visual J++. Refer to your top five sites often as things change and improve.

Extension

A. Open your browser.

B. Find and bookmark your five most valuable resources or Web pages on Java and Visual J++.

C. Search the Web for an additional Web page that uses Java in an interesting way.

D. Bookmark that Web page also.

E. When you have finished, close your browser.

Building Java Applets with Visual J++

There are special tools to help programmers create applets in Java. These tools are called **integrated development environments**. These development environments put many software tools together in a nice neat software package on your personal computer. This means that as you start to program, you have all the support you need to be successful.

This book uses the popular Visual J++ from Microsoft. Microsoft calls its integrated development environment by the name *Developer Studio*. In addition to helping Java programmers, Microsoft has created versions of its Developer Studio to help C++ and Visual Basic programmers. When you learn to use Visual J++ Developer Studio, you will already know a lot about how to use the Visual C++ and Visual Basic Developer Studios.

This section gets you started creating programs using Visual J++. You will create simple programs that will demonstrate the features of Visual J++'s Developer Studio and the fundamentals of Java programming.

You will learn to manipulate data, information, and variables. You will use object-oriented programming (OOP) in the activities. As you manipulate various tools in the Developer Studio, you will see how many of a programmer's tasks can be simplified by using the **Applet Wizards** in Visual J++.

Sector 2

In Chapter 3 *The Visual J++ Developer Studio* will give you a tour of Microsoft's tools for Java development. You will learn how easy it is to install Visual J++ on your computer and use the studio to create and modify simple applets. You will also learn the six steps in the Java programming process.

In Chapter 4 *Creating Java Source Code* lets you experience what programming in Java is really like. Learning to write and manipulate code will develop your understanding of Java language basics. All the applets that you create can be viewed with your Java-enabled browser.

The Visual J++ Developer Studio

Good things come in boxes. (Pizza comes in boxes!) Every programmer knows that the Visual J++ development environment also comes in a box. To a programmer, Visual J++ is better than pizza.

The Microsoft Visual J++ Developer Studio has all sorts of tools to help create exciting applets, including:

- Helpful **Applet Wizards**

- A **ClassView** feature

- The Visual J++ "just-in-time" compiler

- A visual debugger

- The Internet Explorer Web browser

In this chapter you will learn to install Visual J++ and use the Developer Studio to create simple applets. You will also learn to modify applets. In the process of learning to use the Developer Studio software, you will be introduced to the Java language and the six-step programming process used to create Java applets.

O b j e c t i v e s :

- Name the parts of the Developer Studio interface.
- List the six steps of the Java programming process.
- Create a Java folder for your Java projects.
- Install the Visual J++ Developer Studio.
- Create a Java project.
- Write simple Java source code.
- Compile your source code while automatically creating an HTML page.
- View applets in the Internet Explorer.
- Create a simple Java applet with the Applet Wizard.

A Java Development Environment

The early days of Java programming were far from simple.

Because Java was a new programming language, Java didn't have a development environment. A **development environment** is a set of software programs used to create other software programs.

In early Java, programmers had to piece together all of the various components required to create Java applets, including:

- A **text editor** or a **source code editor** for typing Java text
- An **HTML editor** for creating the HTML code needed to carry the Java <APPLET> code
- A group of Java **classes**
- A **compiler**
- A Java **debugger**
- A Java **viewer** with a Java **bytecode translator**, or a **Web browser** with a Java **interpreter**

Whew! This list of tools can be confusing. Imagine trying to find each element listed above and making them work together effectively. Fortunately, you can forget about having to search for the many Java tools you need to do the job.

With the release of **Microsoft's Visual J++ Developer Studio** in September of 1996, you can now find all of the tools listed above in one convenient software program. The Developer Studio is a complete Java development environment – with all the tools you need in one spot.

Introducing the Microsoft Visual J++ Developer Studio

The Visual J++ Developer Studio (Figure 3.1) is an award-winning Java development environment. Specifically, **Visual J++** is a suite of software development tools that focuses on creating Java <APPLETS> for the World Wide Web.

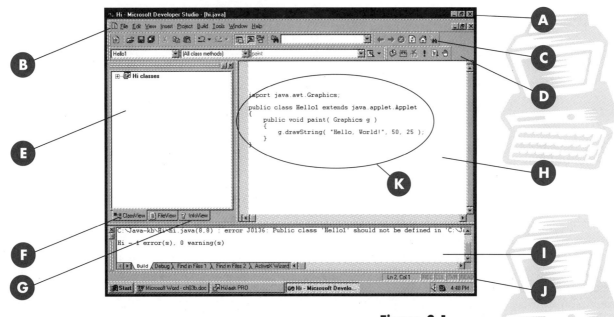

Figure 3.1

The code shown in the editing window reads:

```
import java.awt.Graphics;
public class Hello1 extends java.applet.Applet
{
    public void paint( Graphics g )
    {
        g.drawString( "Hello, World!", 50, 25 );
    }
}
```

The build/output window reads:

```
C:\Java-kb\Hi\hi.java(8,8) : error J0136: Public class 'Hello1' should not be defined in 'C:\Ja
Hi - 1 error(s), 0 warning(s)
```

Figure 3.1
The Microsoft Developer Studio Screen
A – Title bar,
B – Menu bar,
C – Standard Toolbar,
D – Project Toolbar,
E – Project Workspace,
F – ClassView tab,
G – InfoView tab,
H – Editing window,
I – Build/Output window,
J – Status bar,
K – Source code appears in different colors

In this chapter you will create Java applets using the Java language. To make it easier for you to learn Java, you will use the Microsoft Visual J++ Developer Studio. As you begin completing activities, you will see the following advantages of using Microsoft's Visual J++ Developer Studio:

- The Visual J++ Developer Studio is visual! Key Java code is displayed in different colors so you can see what you are creating. (See Figure 3.1). This color coding will help you recognize when you have typed an instruction incorrectly. It also helps you distinguish between different types of Java statements.
- The Visual J++ Developer Studio has many powerful features including an internal text editor, debugger, compiler, linker, and an Applet Wizard that takes care of several separate programming tasks.
- The Developer Studio is based upon the very successful Visual C++ Developer Studio. So, while the Visual J++ Studio is new, professional programmers have tested its basic features for years. If you learn to use the Visual J++ Developer Studio, using the Visual C++ Developer Studio will seem like coming home to familiar ground.
- Visual J++ compiles your source code into bytecode programs that run on the Java Virtual Machine. This may sound complicated, but it really isn't. Rather than create software that will only run on a single type of computer, Visual J++ compiles bytecodes for an imaginary computer called the **Java Virtual Machine** or **JVM**. Then, the Java-enabled browser interprets the JVM bytecodes and converts them to run on the specific computer or machine the applet user is using.

Why does Visual
J++ display words
in different colors?

V isual J++ is
color coded for your
protection! The color
green is used for
//Comments. Blue is
used to highlight com-
piler directives or com-
mands Visual J++ uses
to create bytecodes.
Black is used for other
information such as
class definitions and
variables. You will
learn more about these
different parts of a
Java program in
Activities 4 and 5.

The Parts of the Developer Studio

Examine Figure 3.1 for some of the key parts of the Visual J++ Developer Studio:

- Title bar
- Menu bar
- Standard toolbar
- Project toolbar
- Project workspace
- ClassView tab
- InfoView tab
- Editing window
- Build/Output window
- Status bar
- Source code that appears in different colors

Hidden behind all of the buttons, menus, and tabs are a host of powerful software tools that will aid you in your Java programming.

Java Development Process

Creating Java applets requires knowing about the Java development process. This process is made easier by the Developer Studio which makes going step by step a natural thing to do. The Java development process has six steps:

1. Begin a Visual J++ project.

2. Write Java source code.

3. Build the applet.

4. Debug the applet.

5. Execute the applet.

6. View the applet in action.

Step 1: Begin a Visual J++ Project

Before you start to create any Java applet, you must first define the Java **project**. A **project file** describes all of the files associated with a project. The project file is like defining a list of ingredients used in a recipe.

Using the pizza analogy, assume someone calls and orders a combination pizza with all the toppings. The ingredients list for a combination pizza could be:

- Pizza crust
- Pizza sauce

- Three types of cheese
  - American
  - Mozzarella
  - Provolone
- Seven toppings
  - Pepperoni
  - Ham
  - Pineapple
  - Mushrooms
  - Sausage
  - Peppers
  - Onions

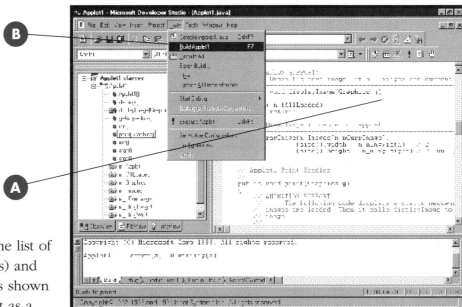

While not nearly as tasty, the list of Java project objects (or classes) and methods can be quite long, as shown in Figure 3.2. Think of this list as a list of ingredients in a recipe to make applets.

Every Visual J++ Java applet must have its project components defined in a special project file.

Figure 3.2
A Java Project File
A – This is the list of ingredients that will be used to create the spinning world applet in Activity 6,
B – Select the Build option to start mixing the ingredients together!

Step 2: Write Java Source Code

After you have defined the Java project, you can begin writing Java **source code**. All Java programming begins with the creation of source code. Source code is just what it sounds like, the source information that dictates everything that the applet is supposed to do or accomplish.

In a sense, source code is like a cooking recipe. It is a step-by-step guide telling the Visual J++ compiler how to make an applet. If you get the right recipe, Visual J++ will follow your instructions to the letter and the outcome will be fantastic. However, your source code must be correct before Visual J++ can do its job.

Source code is a series of words and symbols. This Java-speak looks very strange to the outsider, but Java programmers quickly learn the meaning of each character, name, and symbol. Source code contains the essential information the Java compiler needs (see Step 3) to create a Java applet.

Figure 3.3 shows a sample of source code for the "Hello, World Wide Web!" program. It is adapted from one of the most fundamental of beginner programs called "Hello, World!" This is the first programming project in most

```
import java.awt.Graphics;
    class Hello extends java.applet.Applet
    {
        public void paint ( Graphics g )
        {
            g.drawString ( "Hello, World Wide Web!", 50, 25 )
        }
    }
```

Figure 3.3
Source code for "Hello,
World Wide Web!

programming classes.

Yes, source code is funny looking. But every symbol and every word denotes a particular command or method that the Developer Studio will use to create or compile a Java applet.

Believe it or not, even the punctuation is important. The semicolon (;) at the end of Graphics in the first line is essential. The squiggly parentheses {called curly braces} are essential in telling the Java compiler when to begin, stop, and start a new operation or **method**. Even the commas between the numbers are important in the compilation of Java source code.

Step 3: Build the Applet (Compiling and Linking Source Code)

The Visual J++ compiler builds software from source code. The compiler is the most powerful piece of software inside the Developer Studio.

What a compiler does is best explained with another pizza analogy. A compiler is like a pizza oven. While the source code <APPLET> *recipe* dictates step-by-step, ingredient-by-ingredient how the pizza is to be made, the *oven* compiler cooks the pizza to perfection. Compilers take the source code ingredients and turn them into a hot, spicy pizza <APPLET> for someone to enjoy.

To use a more technical explanation, a Java compiler interprets the source code, then churns the source code commands into a product called **byte-codes**. These bytecodes are the substance inside a Java applet.

Bytecodes are hideously complicated. To look at them is enough to scare even the most seasoned Java programmer. If a programmer had to write Java programs in bytecodes, they would spend a thousand times longer creating the same applet.

After compilation, the Developer Studio must link the bytecode to all the separate files and components (called classes) the program needs to run successfully. Linking is an important part of the building process.

The oven compiler

The source code recipe

The programmer chef

Step 4: Debug the Applet

As every pizza chef can tell you, there are always a few bugs in every kitchen. Before you can finish your software, you must get the bugs out!

It is a very rare day that a Java developer (another word for a Java programmer) gets everything right the first time. Just like writing a school essay, it takes a few revisions to get it right.

In long programs, finding the errors can be difficult. Fortunately, there is a tool in the Developer Studio that can help find the errors. This tool is called the **debugger**.

The Visual J++ debugger has the job of finding errors in a Java program. The debugger works a lot like a spell and grammar checker in a word processing program. A spell checker looks for possible misspelled or duplicate words, and a grammar checker evaluates the syntax of a sentence for errors or mistakes. For example, is there a noun in each sentence? Is there a verb? Does each sentence end with a period, question mark, or exclamation point?

Java source code must follow Java spelling and grammar rules called Java **syntax**. Debuggers make sure these rules are followed and give the Java developer the chance to identify and fix the problems before they crash the Java applet.

The Visual J++ debugger runs automatically and identifies problems in Java applets on the fly–quickly pointing out syntax and other logic errors in the Java source and bytecode.

Step 5: Execute the Applet

When programmers write application software in other languages, C++ for example, they create source code and compile it just like you will do in Java. There are, however, some important differences between other programming languages and Java. Other programming languages generally create **applications** or **executables** that "run native" on a particular kind of computer. These applications, or executables, are created for specific computers, like the Intel Pentium processor found in many Windows computers, or the Motorola 604 Power PC processor commonly found in Macintosh computers.

Java is platform independent. **Platform independence** means that Java applets can run on any computer. The programmer can compile the code once, ship it on a Web page to any computer in the world, and in theory, that computer can run the application. Platform independence allows Java applets to ride the Web.

However, to make platform independence possible, each computer must have a Java interpreter that can read the compiled Java applet's bytecode and convert it into the specific language the computer understands.

The trick is getting rid of the bugs before they end up in your pizza!

FAQs

What is bytecode?

Bytecode is the stuff that applets are made of. If you have an applet, you have bytecode. This bytecode is interpreted by a Java-enabled Web browser. Once the applet's bytecodes have been translated by the interpreter, the program runs.

FAQs

What is syntax?

Syntax refers to the orderly and systematic arrangement of Java words, symbols, methods, or expressions. A syntax error is like a grammar or punctuation error in English or Italian. Syntax errors include placing the Java commands in the wrong order, misspelling a Java method, or using the wrong Java words or punctuation.

To view applets from the Web you need a Java-enabled browser, because Web applets are not written for any single type of computer. The secret to Java's portability lies in the Java Virtual Machine (JVM). Java applets are compiled by Visual J++ to run on a make believe (virtual) computer. This virtual computer defines everything the applet can do. Then, a translator takes the definitions developed by the JVM and interprets them to the definitions that a real computer— Macintosh, Windows, or Unix—understands.

Another food example may help. Suppose you venture out to a fancy Italian restaurante, Il Restoranti Appletto, for example. You walk in, sit down, and open the menu. To your surprise, the entire menu is in Italian, and you don't speak Italian. Fortunately, Senore Appletto speaks perfect Italian and translates the menu to English for you. You don't need to be able to read the menu if you have a **translator** like Senore Appletto. In the same way, a Java interpreter can read Java bytecode and can translate the bytecodes into a language the specific computer can understand.

Java interpreters are built into Java browsers. This is why the Microsoft Visual J++ Developer Studio installs the Internet Explorer browser. This browser has a built-in Java applet interpreter that translates your compiled bytecodes into a language your computer understands. (See Figure 3.4.)

Step 6: View the Applet on a Web Page

Applets require an HTML Web page before they can be picked up by a Web browser and interpreted. Therefore, a basic understanding of HTML is required in order to display applets properly on the Web.

However, the Developer Studio will allow you to test your applets in the Internet Explorer without knowing HTML. The Developer Studio will automatically create the minimal HTML tags necessary to display and run the Java applet on a simple HTML Web page. The HTML code created by the Developer Studio is simple, but it gets the job done, allowing you to view, run, and test your applets. You get a chance to see how your applet will look on the World Wide Web.

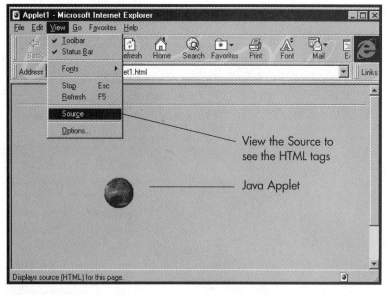

Figure 3.4
The Internet Explorer browser interprets Java bytecode.

Basic HTML codes required to display Java applets include the following tags:

<HTML></HTML>	Starts and stops an HTML document.
<TITLE></TITLE>	Places a title at the top of the Web browser.
<BODY></BODY>	Defines the information to be displayed in a browser display window.
<APPLET></APPLET>	Defines the beginning and end of a Java applet.

Figure 3.5 shows you a sample of the HTML tags the Developer Studio creates before it displays your applet in the Internet Explorer.

Debriefing

In this chapter you learned many new terms. Visit the Glossary online to look up words you don't understand. The glossary is part of the Studio-JPlus site. Access the site through your favorites or bookmarks list.

In the activities that follow, you will use the six steps in the Java applet programming process. These steps are:

1. Begin a Visual J++ project.

2. Write Java source code.

3. Build the applet.

4. Debug the applet.

5. Execute the applet.

6. View the applet in action.

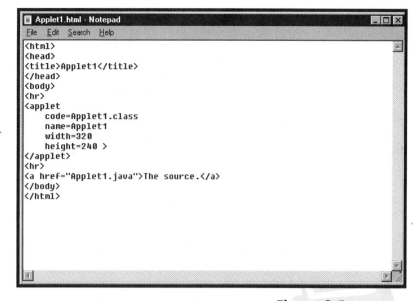

Figure 3.5
The HTML Source

Watch carefully as you move from step to step. The Visual J++ Developer Studio accomplishes its job so quickly that you may miss important steps if you blink or run to the phone to order a pizza!

Take a Test!

Review the terms and questions in your online reading guide. Then, journey down the information superhighway to Studio-JPlus and take the Chapter 3 test. Use your favorites or bookmark list to access the Studio-JPlus site.

List of Terms

Applets
Applet Wizard
Applications
Bytecode
Classes
ClassView
Compiler
Debugger
Development environment
Executables
HTML Editor
Interpreter
Java Virtual Machine (JVM)
Visual J++
Method
Platform independence
Plug-in
Project
Project file
Run native
Source code
Source code editor
Syntax
Text editor
Translator
Viewer
Web browser

Just Click Next, Next, Next, . . .

You may be in a situation where you don't need to worry about installing the Visual J++ Developer Studio. However, at some point you may need to download and install an update, or reinstall your software for some reason or another. At that time, you will find this activity very helpful.

This activity walks you through the process of installing Visual J++. It is as easy as clicking next, next, and next. There are a few installation decisions you will want to make. We will help you with those decisions as you proceed.

Before you begin, you need to be able to answer "yes" to the following minimum configuration questions:

- Do you have a 486 or higher processor?
- Does your computer use Windows 95 or Window NT Workstation 4.0 or higher?
- Do you have at least 8 MB of memory?
- Do you have at least 25MB or more of free hard drive space?
- Do you have a VGA or higher monitor?
- Do you have a CD-ROM drive?
- Do you have a mouse?

If the answer to each question above is "yes" then you have the minimum computer configuration you need to install and run the Visual J++ Developer Studio. Remember, this is a minimum configuration. The following computer system would run the program much faster:

- A Pentium processor
- 12 to 16 megs of memory
- 50 MB of hard drive space
- A Super VGA monitor

Still, even with a minimum system, you can create some great applets.

O b j e c t i v e s :

- Learn about the minimum configuration for Visual J++
- Install Visual J++

Step 1: To install Visual J++, start your computer.

Step 2: Insert the Microsoft Visual J++ CD into the CD drive.

//Important Comment: If this is a first time installation, your computer may take over and start the installation process automatically. In this case, the Setup window will appear and you can skip to Step 3. If the Setup screen does not appear, continue with Step 2A.

2A: Click the **Start** button, select **Settings**, then choose **Control Panel**.

2B: Double-click on the **Add/Remove Programs** option.

2C: Select **Install** from the Add/Remove Programs dialog box as marked in Figure A4.1.

Figure A4.1
The Add/Remove
Programs Dialog Box
A – Click Install

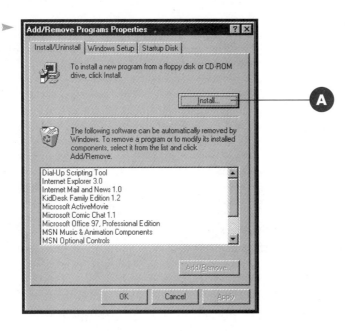

2D: Follow the instructions you are given. When you come to the Run Installation Program dialog box, browse until you find the D:\setup.exe program as marked in Figure A4.2.

Hint! Windows will probably find D:\setup.exe for you!

Figure A4.2
The Run Installation
Program Dialog Box
A – Browser to
D:\setup.exe

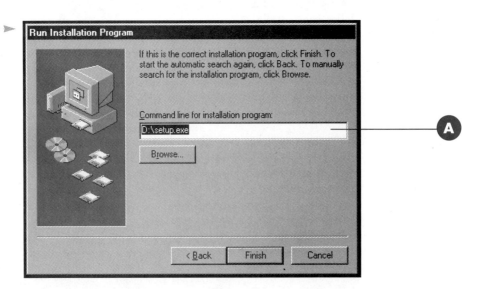

2E: Click the **Finish** button.

Step 3: To install the Visual J++ Developer Studio:

3A: When the Visual J++ Master Setup Dialog box appears, click **Install Visual J++** as shown in Figure A4.3.

Figure A4.3
Install Visual J++

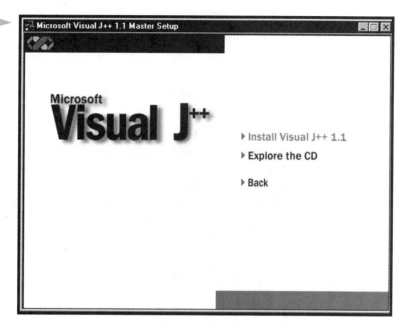

3B: Follow the instructions on the screen. For the most part, all you need to do is read the screen and click **Next**.

3C: When you come to the Registration dialog box, you will be asked to enter some specific data and information. Enter the following information as shown in Figure A4.4:

1. User Name:
2. Organization:
3. CD Key (Note: The CD key is found on a sticker on the back of your Visual J++ CD.)
4. Press **Next**.

Figure A4.4
The Registration Dialog
Box
A – User Name
B – Organization
C – CD Ke,
D – Press Next

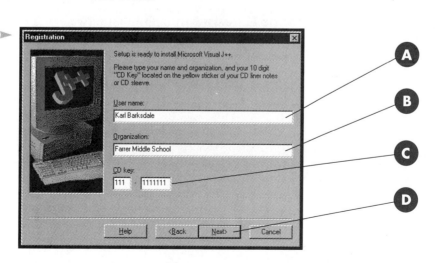

3D: The next screen is the most important. You need to make some decisions about the kind of install that you want to use from the list of choices. To make all the choices you must know how much memory is available on your computer's hard drive. If you have plenty of MB of storage space available, click on the **Typical** button and click **Next**. If you don't have a lot of storage space available on your hard drive, select one of the other options. If you need to know more about each option, click the **Help** button. (See Figure A4.5.)

Figure A4.5
Installation Options

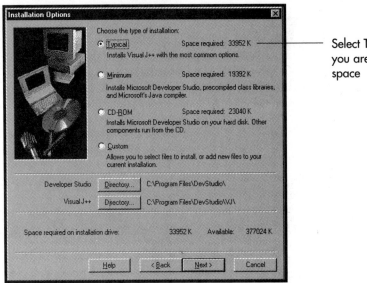

Select Typical Install unless you are low on hard drive space

3E: The next few screens give you lots of information, so kick back, read the screens, (or catch a few zzzzzz's) and wait until you are prompted again. You will be asked to click **Next** a few times, so keep your mouse handy.

3F: Make sure you install the Internet Explorer on your computer. When prompted, click **Install**.

3G: You may want to register your copy of Visual J++. If you have a modem, when the Register Visual J++ dialog box appears, click the **Online Registration** button. Otherwise, click **OK** and continue your installation.

3H: Before your installation can be totally complete, you must restart Windows as it directs in Figure A4.6. Click the **Restart Windows** button.

Figure A4.6
Restart Windows Dialog
Box
A – Click Restart
Windows

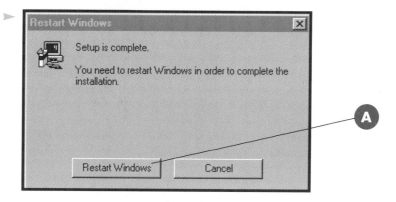

3I: As your computer restarts, the Internet Explorer starts and gives you the welcome message shown in Figure A4.7. When you are done reading, click the Close box to continue.

Figure A4.7
Internet Explorer's
Welcome Message
A – Click the close box

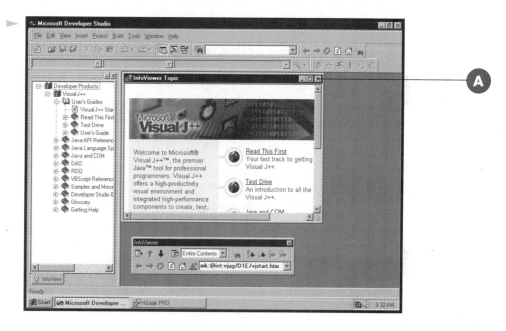

Note: You can also click on the J in the picture and you will be taken directly to Microsoft's Web page. A cool trick!

Debriefing

Installing the Visual J++ Developer Studio is very easy. The main thing is to remember to click **Next** when prompted. Still, there are some important steps that require a little decision making. For example:

- Make sure you know how much storage space you have on your hard drive.
- Make sure your computer meets the minimum specifications.
- Keep your CD case handy so you can look up your CD key number.

Hello, World Wide Web, It's Me!

With Visual J++ installed, you are ready to create your first Java applet. Since the first programming course taught in ancient Greece by Aristotle in the year 350 B.C., programmers have been obliged to write the "Hello, World!" program. This first program has a long-standing tradition.

Frankly, "Hello, World!" is overused. Nevertheless, you don't dare become the first programmer in history not to write "Hello, World!" So, we are going to compromise. We will create "Hello, World Wide Web!" simply and painlessly using the Visual J++ Developer Studio.

Before you begin, you should create a folder or subdirectory to store all of your Java projects. This is important, especially if you are sharing a computer with other students. By placing all of your Java projects in one folder, they will be easy to find.

O b j e c t i v e s :

- Create a Java projects folder.
- Start the Visual J++ Developer Studio.
- Learn to use the online learning tools.
- Begin your first Java project.
- Create "Hello, World Wide Web!"
- View your first Java applet in the Internet Explorer browser.
- Save your finished project.
- Exit the Visual J++ Developer Studio.

Step 1: To create a folder for your Java projects:

1A: Double-click your computer icon as shown in Figure A5.1.

1B: Double-click your hard drive icon.

1C: Click **File**.

1D: Click **New**.

1E: Select **Folder** as shown in Figure A5.1.

Creating an Applet the Old-Fashioned Way

Activity 5

Figure A5.1
Creating a JAVA-??
Folder
A – Double-click computer icon
B – Open your hard drive
C – Select File
D – Pick New,
E – Click Folder

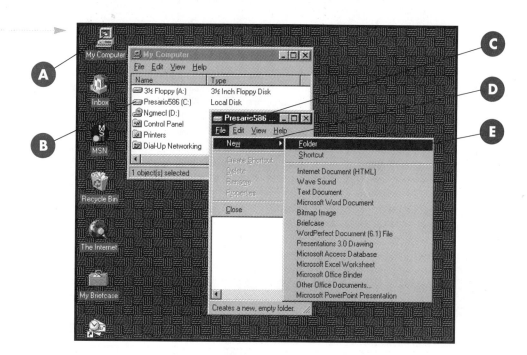

1F: Name your folder Java-??. The ?? is for your initials.

 //**Comment:** Kal Bumgardner and Karl Barksdale would type **Java-kb**, while Jay Stephens would be **Java-js**. (See Figure A5.2.) If you have the same initials as another student, include your middle initial or add a number after your initials. The main thing is to have your own folder in which to save your work.

Figure A5.2
Name your folder Java-??
A – Replace ?? with your initials

Note: Using your initials can be important if many people use the same computer.

Step 2: To start the Visual J++ Developer Studio:

FAQs

What is the difference between folder, directory, and subdirectory?

Not much.
A folder is a Windows 95 and a Macintosh term used for directories. A subdirectory is simply a directory inside another directory, or in Windows 95, a folder inside a folder could be called a subdirectory.

2A Click the **Start** button.

2B: Select **Programs**.

2C: Click on the **Microsoft Visual J++** menu item.

2D: Click on the **Microsoft Developer Studio** icon. (See Figure A5.3.)

Figure A5.3
Start your Visual J++
Developer Studio
A – Click Start,
B – Click Programs,
C – Select Microsoft
Visual J++,
D – Click Microsoft
Developer Studio

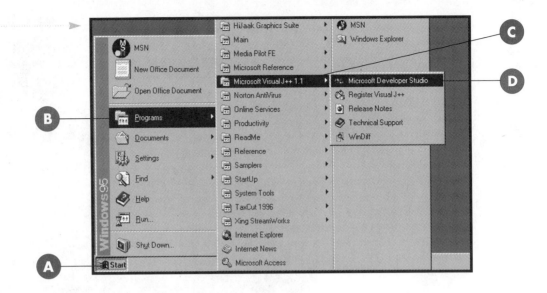

 //Comment: When the Studio is first opened, you may see a Tips of the Day window. The tips are helpful and explain many of the hidden features of the Visual J++ Studio. If you want to continue viewing these handy tips every time you start Visual J++, place a check mark as indicated in Figure A5.4. Click Close when you are ready to continue.

Figure A5.4
The Tips Window

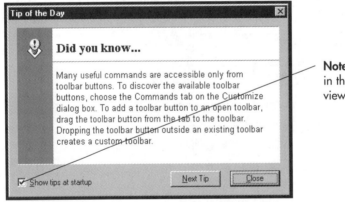

Note: Click a check mark in the box to continue viewing the Tips windows.

Step 3: To find instructions on how to create a Java applet:

3A: After the Visual J++ Master Setup dialog box appears, click on the **InfoView** tab as marked in Figure A5.5.

3B: Click on the **+** signs starting with the **Developer Products** icon, moving down to the **Visual J++** icon, **User's Guides**, and then the **Read This First** information. Finally, open the **Installing Visual J++** icon as shown in Figure A5.5.

3C: Double-click on the **Creating a Simple Java Applet** article. Review the steps in the article. Look at the sample code. Does it look like a foreign language? It's called Java-speak!

//Comment: You can print the "Creating a Simple Java Applet" article by selecting **Print** from the **File** menu. You can also follow the steps outlined in the "Creating a Simple Java Applet" article and write an applet of your own. If you need additional help with pictures, go to Step 4 and follow along with the text.

Figure A5.5
The InfoView
A – Click the InfoView tab.
B – Click the + signs,
C – Double-click Creating a Simple Java Applet,
D – Read the instructions,
Note: Print from File menu.

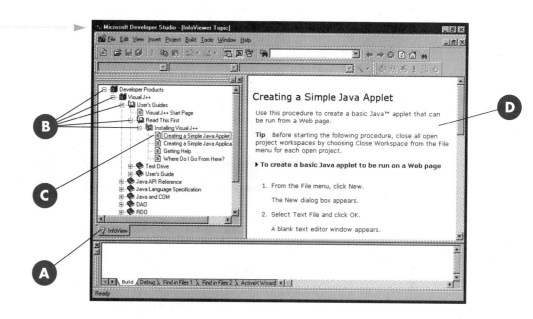

> **Step 4:** To create the "Hello, World Wide Web!" applet:
>
> **4A:** Click **New** from the **File** menu as shown in Figure A5.6.

Figure A5.6
The File menu
A – Click New

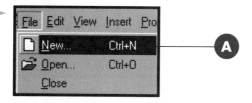

4B: Click on the **Files** tab.

4C: Select **Text File** from the **New** dialog box as shown in Figure A5.7.

4D: Click **OK**.

Figure A5.7
The New dialog box
B – Click File tab,
C – Select Text File,
D – Click OK

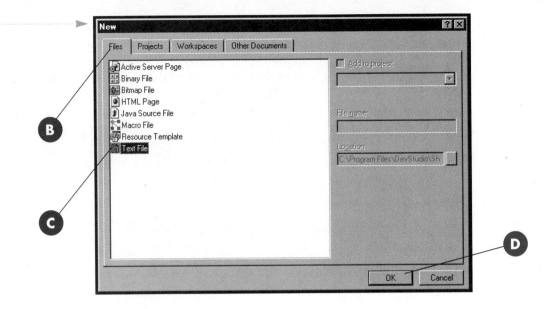

4E: Enter the code shown below and in Figure A5.8 into the text editor in Visual J++.

//Comment: When you key your source code, use the **Tab** key to indent, press **Enter** at the end of each line, and use **Shift+Tab** to move your cursor to the left margin of the Editing Window.

```
import java.awt.Graphics;
class Hello1 extends java.applet.Applet
{
    public void paint( Graphics g )
    {
        g.drawString( "Hello, World Wide Web!", 50, 25 );
    }
}
```

Figure A5.8
Saving Your Source Code
E – Key in your source code,
F – Click Save As

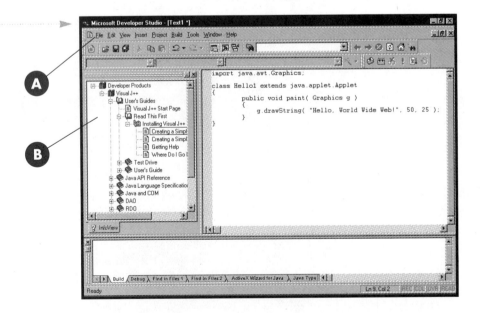

4F: Select **Save As** from the **File** menu.

4G: Find the Java-?? folder in which you want to save your files.

4H: Enter the name **Hello1.java** in the File name field as shown in Figure A5.9. (Make sure you capitalize the H in **Hello1.java**.)

Figure A5.9:
The File menu
G – Find your Java-??
folder
H – Type Hello1.java
I – Click Save

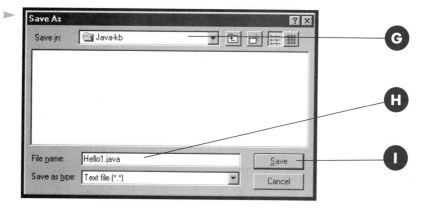

4I: Click **Save**.

4J: Select **Compile Hello1.java** from the **Build** menu as in Figure A5.10.

Figure A5.10:
The Build Menu
J – Click Compile Hello

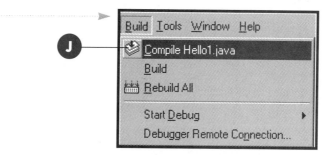

//Comment: Visual J++ will then pop up with a series of questions it needs answered before it can create your applet. First, it will ask you to create a project workspace. Select **Yes** to create a default workspace (meaning J++ will set up for you). (See Figure A5.11.)

Figure A5.11:
Create a Project
Workspace

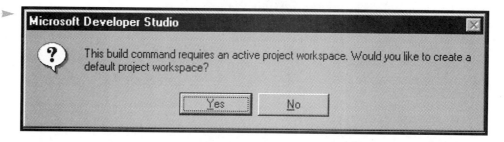

//Comment: The class view window will appear asking for a name for your class. Enter **Hello1** as shown in Figure A5.12. Click the + signs to see the various classes and methods. These will be discussed in Chapter 4.

4K: Select **Execute** from the **Build** menu as marked in Figure A5.12.

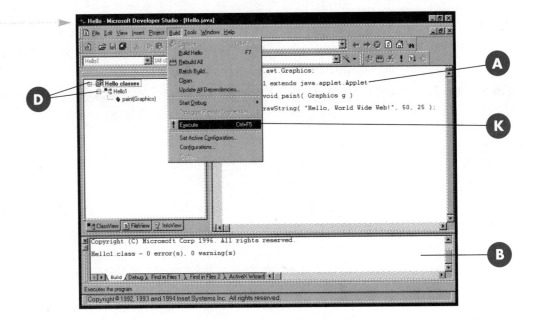

 //Comment: Watch as your code compiles in the window at the bottom of your screen.

 Debug: If you have errors, go back to your source code and look for any mistakes you may have made, including using a colon (:) instead of a semi-colon (;) and a bracket ([) instead of a curly brace ({). Every word, symbol, and space counts for something and must be correct.

4L: Select **Execute** from the **Build** menu as marked in Figure A5.

4M: Visual J++ will then ask you to create a **Class** file name for this file. Enter *Hello1* in the Class file name box as shown in Figure A5.13. (Make sure you capitalize the H in Hello1.)

4N: Click **OK**.

Figure A5.13
Information for Running
Class Dialog Box
A – Enter Hello1, Use a
capital H in Hello1,
B – Click OK

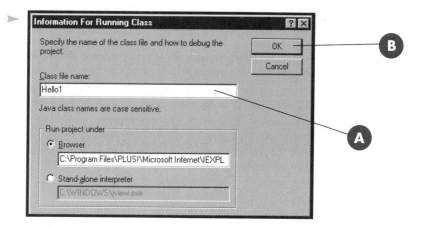

40: If everything is correct, your program will be displayed in the Internet Explorer as it appears in Figure A5.14:

Figure A5.14
Your Java applet as it
appears in the Internet
Explorer browser
A – This is your applet
running

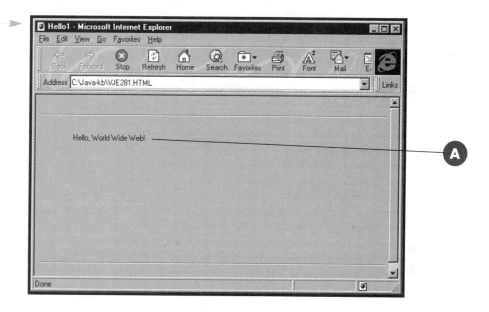

Step 5: Close the Internet Explorer and exit Visual J++.

Debriefing

You have just finished creating the "Hello, World Wide Web!" applet. In doing so, you have created the **Hello1.java** class. In that class you have used a method call paint( ) to literally paint the words "Hello, World Wide Web!" across the screen. Methods and classes will be explained in more detail in Chapter 4.

To see the **Hello1.java** class and the paint( ) method:

1. Start the Microsoft Visual J++ Developer Studio as you did in Step 2.

2. If this was the last applet created in Visual J++, it will appear automatically. If not, you will have to open by using Open on the **File** menu.

Look in your Java-?? folder to find **Hello1.java**. You may have to change the File type to Java files.

3.   Click the + button as marked in Figure A5.12. The Java class you created called **Hello1** will appear.

4.   Click the + button as marked in Figure A5.12. The Java command **paint( )**, which is called a method, will appear. The **paint( )** command is the method that makes the words "Hello, World Wide Web!" paint or appear on the screen. Look for how it is used in the next activity.

5.   Close the Internet Explorer and exit Visual J++.

Spin Around the Studio

Admit it. The "Hello, World Wide Web!" applet you created in Activity 5 (while a timeless variation on a classic beginner program) was boring!

Java does not have to be so dull. Java is an object-oriented programming language. This means that classes are built into the Developer Studio to create certain "objects" for you. You don't have to write any Java source code to take advantage of these classes.

Let's create an applet using the Applet Wizard available with Microsoft's Visual J++. The result will be something much more interesting than "Hello World Wide Web!"

O b j e c t i v e s :

- Start the Visual J++ Developer Studio.
- Find the Applet Wizard features.
- Experiment with Applet Wizards.
- Create a spinning world using Applet Wizards.
- View the code that creates the dialog box.
- View the spinning world in the Internet Explorer.
- Save your finished project.
- Exit the Visual J++ Developer Studio.

> **Step 1:** Start Visual J++.

 //Comments: Revisit Activity 5 if you need help starting Visual J++.

> **Step 2:**

To create a new Visual J++ project:

2A: Click on the **File** menu.

2B: Select **New**.

2C: Select the **Projects** tab as shown in Figure A6.1.

Figure A6.1
Projects Tab
C – Select Projects tab
D – Select Java Applet
Wizard
E – Select your Java-??
Folder
F – Enter Applet1
G – Click OK

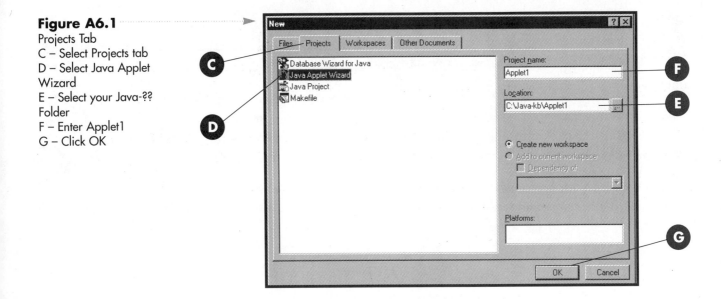

2D: Select **Java Applet Wizard**.

2E: In the **Location** field, select your *Java-??* folder or subdirectory.

2F: Click the **Name** field and enter **Applet1**. (Remember to capitalize the first letter in Applet1.)

2G: Click **OK**.

Creating an Applet

Programs created in Java can run either as applications or as applets. Applets can be run on a Web page. Applications can run as stand-alone software programs. In this book, we will concentrate on applets.

To create an applet:

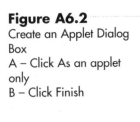 **Step 3:**

Figure A6.2
Create an Applet Dialog Box
A – Click As an applet only
B – Click Finish

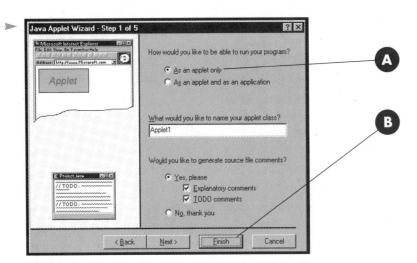

3A: Click **As an applet only** as shown in Figure A6.2.

3B: Click the **Finish** button.

3C: Click **OK**.

> **Step 4:** Your computer may make some funny sounds and then "presto" you have an applet.

To open and view the applet classes and methods:

Figure A6.3
Look At the Wizard's
Code
A – Click +,
B – Click +,
C – Double-click
paint(Graphics),
D – View Method,
E – Watch the code compile here,
F – Select Build Applet1

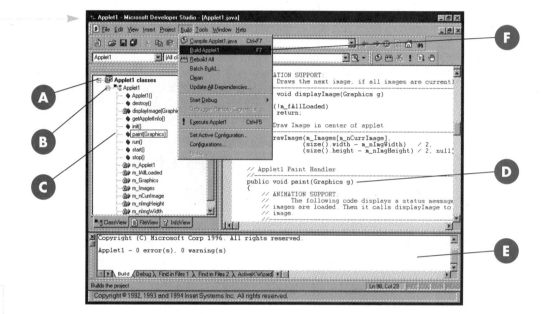

FAQs

What is Presto?

resto is from the Italian word "praesto" which means ready. The French say viola! We might substitute "cool." Presto is something you would say if you were to wave a magic wand and turn rocks into gold or pull a rabbit out of a hat. Presto is also something you would say when your applet or your pizza is ready.

4A: Click on the + sign to the left of your **Applet1 classes** as shown in Figure A6.3.

Note: You should now see another + sign along with some multicolored boxes and word *Applet1*. This *Applet1* is a class the wizard has created for you.

4B: Click on the + sign to the left of the Applet1 class.

//Comment: Before the next step, take a deep breath. You are now going to get a good look at some real live, heavy-duty Java code in the editing window as shown in Figure A6.3.

4C: Place your cursor on the paint(Graphics) method and double-click.

4D: Your cursor should be flashing just to the left of a funny-looking line which says something to the effect of "public void paint (Graphics g)" as marked in Figure A6.3.

//Comment: Scroll down the editing window and look for the same g.drawString command you used in your *Hello1* applet. Looks like this command is used quite a bit in programming.

Step 5: To build or compile your Java code:

   5A: Click the **Build** menu.

   5B: Select **Build Applet1**.

   5C: Watch your Java applet compile in the build window as shown in Figure A6.3.

   5D: Click on the **Build** menu and select **Execute Applet1** as shown in Figure A6.4.

Figure 6.4
The Build Menu
A – Click Build,
B – Select Build Applet
D – Select Execute
Applet1

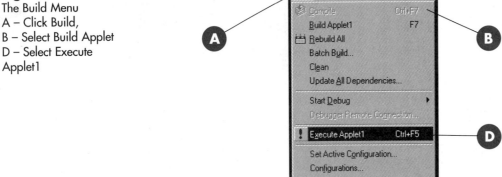

Now, sit back and inspect your work. J++ should automatically take you into Internet Explorer where you will see the phrase "Loading images" displayed on the screen. Then presto — a spinning world will appear as shown in Figure A6.5. Congratulations!!! You have just created a Java applet using Visual J++'s tools.

Figure A6.5
The Spinning World
Applet

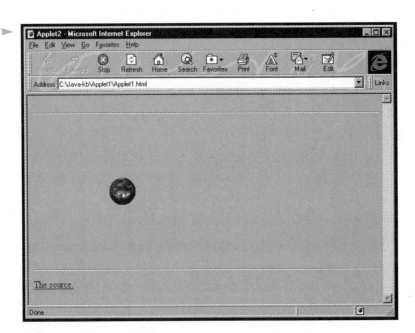

Step 6: Close the Internet Explorer and exit Visual J++.

Debriefing

The Applet Wizard can create a great deal of source code for you quickly. This is often a great way to save time; however, you could enter all the code yourself. As you learn Java, you will find that the Applet Wizards are good-time savers. Careful study of the wizards can also be a great learning tool.

S **low Down the World, I Want to Get Off!**

As a Java programmer, there will be many times when you want to modify the way your applet functions. This requires modifying your source code. For practice, let's modify our spinning globe applet. Have you ever said to yourself, "I just don't have enough time in the day to get everything done?" What if you could slow down time? As you probably noticed in Activity 6, our globe was spinning fairly rapidly. Let's make more time by making our globe turn at a more reasonable rate.

O b j e c t i v e s :

- Modify an existing applet.
- Explain how the frame rate affects animation.

Step 1: Start Visual J++.

Step 2: If the applet1 project appears in the workspace, skip to Step 3. If any other project appears in the workspace, follow the steps below. If the workspace is empty, skip Steps 2A through 2C.

2A: Click on the **File** menu.

2B: Select **Close Workspace**. (See Figure A7.1.)

Figure A7.1
File Menu
A – Close Workspace
menu item

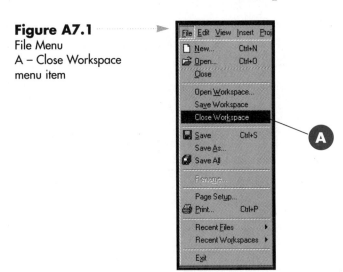

2C: Click **Yes** in response to the question, "Do you want to close all document windows?" (See Figure A7.2.)

Figure A7.2
Dialog box
A – Yes button

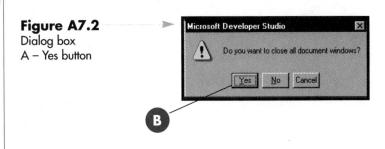

2D: Select **Open Workspace** from the **File** menu.

2E: Browse through the various projects you have created in your Java-?? folder until you find the desired project.

2F: Double-click on the Applet1 folder.

2G: Double-click on the workspace file you want to modify, in this case it would be **Applet1.dsw.**

Step 3: Now that the applet is open, you will modify the rate at which the globe rotates.

3A: In the ClassView window to the left of the workspace, click on the + sign to the left of the Applet1 classes.

3B: Click on the + sign to the left of the Applet1 class.

3C: Double-click on the name of the method you want to modify. In this case you want to modify the **run** method. VJ++ finds the run method in the source code and moves the cursor to the first line of the method. (See Figure A7.3.)

Figure A7.3
Run Method in Source Code
A – Run method in ClassView list
B – Start of source code for run method

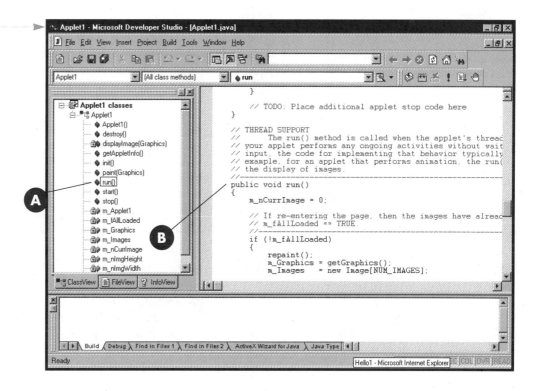

3D: Scroll down in the method until you locate the line that you want to modify. In this case you want to modify the following line:

Thread.sleep(50);

3E: Change the 50 in the Thread.sleep statement to **1000**.

 //Comment: Modifying code often requires some trial and error. Often you have to see the output of an applet on the screen before you know if you've achieved your goal. In this case, you want to slow down your spinning globe. Increasing the number in the statement will slow it down, but it may not be the exact rate you had planned.

3F: Build the modified version of your applet using the steps you learned in Activity 6. (Refer to Activity 6 if you need help.) When VJ++ has completed the build, you should see a 0 errors, 0 warnings message in the docked window at the bottom of the screen. (See Figure A7.4.)

Figure A7.4
Modified Applet after Build
A – Docked Window
B – 0 errors, 0 warnings message

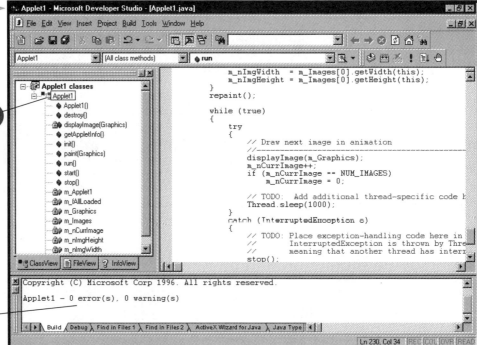

 //Comment: You must rebuild your applet every time you modify it in order for the Visual J++ compiler to recognize the changes you have made to the applet. However, if you do click on the **Execute** option without rebuilding your modified applet, the Visual J++ compiler is smart enough to know that you have modified the source code since the last time you built it. It will then tell you, "One or more files are out of date or do not exist." (See Figure A7.5.)

Figure A7.5
Message for Executing Applet before Building It

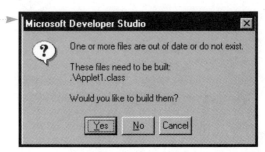

The compiler will show you which files are out of date. An out-of-date file means that something in the file has been modified since the last build. The compiler will ask you, "Would you like to build them?" Click **Yes** in response to this question and your source code will be rebuilt and then executed.

> **Step 4:** Execute the applet.

You should notice that our little globe is turning more slowly. Now if you could only get your hands on that applet in the sky that controls how fast our world turns, you would really make some big bucks as a Java programmer!

To understand the procedure for modifying an existing applet, we suggest that you modify the applet several times by changing the rate at which the world turns. You will notice that the higher the value in the *Thread.sleep(50);* statement, the slower your globe will turn. The lower the value, the faster the world will turn. By changing the value, you are modifying how long your applet waits between displaying the different images of the globe.

Do you remember how a cartoon works? Cartoons are simply a bunch of images of a character flashed before your eyes so quickly that it simulates movement; this is animation. Our globe applet works the same way. There are several images of the globe for each side of the earth. These various images are called **frames** and the time between the display of each frame is called the **frame rate**. By modifying the number in the *Thread.sleep(50)*; statement, you are modifying the frame rate in the applet.

> **Step 5:** Experiment with different rates by changing the *Thread.sleep* statement. Build and execute the applet with each change. When you have finished experimenting, return the statement setting to 1000.

> **Step 6:** Close the Internet Explorer and exit Visual J++.

Debriefing

You have learned how to modify an existing applet to change the way it functions. This new skill will serve you well many times as a Java programmer. You also learned about frames and frame rates. This is important as you begin to learn how to include animation in your applets.

Object-Oriented Programming with Java

Now that you know your way around the Visual J++ Developer Studio, it is time to get down to some serious programming. In this section, you will be introduced to the fundamentals of the Java language.

Remember, Java is an object-oriented programming (OOP) language. To help you better understand OOP, this chapter will introduce you to such Java basics as:

- Java syntax
- Classes
- Methods
- Comments

Visual J++ is often called VJ++. VJ++ was the first integrated development environment for Java. Integrated development environment is just another way of saying that VJ++ gives you all the Java tools you need to create totally cool applets.

Objectives:

- Explain how source code is converted to bytecode.
- Identify classes and objects.
- Define packages.
- Identify methods.
- List the two types of comments found in source code.
- Explain how braces are used in Visual J++.

```
    // Draw Image in center of applet
    //-------------------------------------------------
    g.drawImage(m_Images[m_nCurrImage],
            (size().width - m_nImgWidth)  / 2,
            (size().height - m_nImgHeight) / 2, null);
}

// Great Paint Handler
//-------------------------------------------------
public void paint(Graphics g)
{
    // ANIMATION SUPPORT:
    //      The following code displays a status message until all the
    // images are loaded. Then it calls displayImage to display the current
    // image.
    //-------------------------------------------------
    if (m_fAllLoaded)
    {
        Rectangle r = g.getClipRect();

        g.clearRect(r.x, r.y, r.width, r.height);
        displayImage(g);
    }
}
```

Figure 4.1
Sample of Source Code

FAQs

What is source code?

ource code consists of the basic instructions a programmer creates or "writes." Source code is an essential part of programming. Before a program can be created, a programmer must enter all the specific instructions needed by the compiler. The compiler follows these instructions exactly. Errors in the source code will cause errors when compiling and building the software, and the software will not be created properly.

From Source Code to Bytecode

In Activities 5 and 6 you used Java to create applets. The words and symbols you used represent a language—the language that Visual J++ understands. In Activity 5, you keyed instructions into the VJ++ editing window. The terms and symbols you typed are called **source code**.

Learning Java is Like Learning a Foreign Language

VJ++ converts source code into **bytecodes**. Bytecodes are translated by Web browsers. Converting source code into bytecode takes place in a process called **compiling**. Compiling is done by a compiler. Since Visual J++ is an integrated development environment, it includes a compiler.

In this chapter, you will begin speaking Java more fluently, so you can create a variety of new applets. Just like learning a new language — Italian, French, or Japanese — Java requires learning the following:

- New vocabulary words
- Rules of grammar
- Rules of punctuation
- The structure of words, sentences, and paragraphs

Let's compare Java to Italian:

- Italian has nouns and verbs; Java has classes and methods.
- Italian has pronouns and adjectives; Java has special words that extend and add meaning to Java commands.
- Italian has punctuation marks; Java uses punctuation such as braces and semicolons.
- Italian uses special symbols such as accent marks to aid pronunciation; Java uses symbols with special meaning for the VJ++ compiler.

Java is a really cool written language. Just be glad you don't have to speak Java in bytecodes to a computer! Speaking Java is a job best left to your Visual J++ compiler.

Translating the Java Language

In Activity 5, you wrote the source code shown in Figure 4.2.

```
import java.awt.Graphics;

    class Hello extends java.applet.Applet
    {
        public void paint ( Graphics g )
        {
            g.drawString ( "Hello, World Wide Web!", 50, 25 )
        }
    }
```

We will use this sample and other written source code to begin to learn the Java language. Refer to the source code above as you discover what each piece of the source code does in the program.

Figure 4.2
Hello, World Wide Web
Source Code

Java Grammar Rule #1: Identify the Classes

Object-oriented programming uses classes, or fragments of code to do specific things in a program. These "things" are called **objects**.

Classes are like the nouns in a sentence. Just like you can't have a sentence without a noun, you can't have object-oriented programs without classes. Have you heard the phrase "A noun is a person, place, or thing"? Well, **classes** are things that cause specific action. To be specific, classes are little software programs that can:

- Paint or repaint an image on the screen
- Calculate mathematical functions
- Make a picture or text move across the screen
- Count how many times someone visits a Web page
- Give the time for any time zone in the world

Classes are easy to spot in source code. They have names like Hello and Graphics. They often appear in words separated by dots or periods like java.applet.Applet. You can also find them inside parentheses like (Graphics).

What is the name of the class defined in Figure 4.2? The answer is, of course, Hello.

OOP classes are important for several reasons. First of all, classes allow programmers to avoid having to create everything themselves from scratch. OOP languages like Java provide **reusable code**.

Reusable code includes classes that can be used over and over again. For example, the class **java.awt.Graphics** is essential to most graphics operations and is found in nearly every applet! Its job is to help display graphics and to paint pictures on the browser screen. This class or object

may look fairly simple, but it is actually very complicated. Isn't it nice to know you don't have to create it yourself? You can use it any time you like.

In pizza terms, using the java.awt.Graphics class is like Senore Appletto going to the store and buying all the veggies pre-sliced and ready to throw onto his pizza. Appletto doesn't have to grow all the veggies he needs personally. He just buys the veggies he needs and uses them as he likes.

Java Grammar Rule #2: Identify Packages of Tools You Can Use

There are collections of related classes called **packages**. These packages can be used by the Java programmer to create all kinds of objects. Two examples of packages could be java.applet and java.awt. Both of these packages were used in the "Hello, World Wide Web!" program. Graphics is a class found in the java.awt package. With graphic classes you can create the following objects.

- Oval
- Arc
- Square
- DrawString

Java Grammar Rule #3: Create a Method

Methods define how all the objects, classes, and tools get used! Methods make things happen. Let's analyze how one method, the paint method, is used in the source code for the Hello, World Wide Web applet:

1. **Import** into your source code the Java Abstract Windowing Toolkit with the following command:

   import java.awt.Graphics

2. Later in the source code you will give the **paint** command (also called a **method**):

   Paint (Graphics g)

3. The letter **g** is important. It is called a variable. You must define what a variable does with other commands like this:

   g.drawString

4. The **g.drawString** can then draw the following words within the quotation marks:

   "Hello, World Wide Web!"

Let's look a little closer at the AWT or Abstract Windowing Toolkit. Notice how the word import is used before java.awt.Graphics. If you don't import java.awt.Graphics, you can't use it. Once you import it, you can use it over and over again in your applet.

FAQs

What is the difference between an object and a class?

While the terms are often used interchangeably, there is a technical difference between objects and classes. An object is more of an idea or a concept in the real world. Classes include the actual code that creates the object or idea. Objects are often organized into class libraries. Like books, objects can be checked out and used over and over again.

FAQs

What is AWT?

AWT (as in java.awt.Graphics) stands for Abstract Windowing Toolkit. This toolkit is a package that contains many predefined objects or classes that can help you generate graphics for your applets.

Notice the semicolon (;) at the end of certain lines in the "Hello, World Wide Web" applet. The semicolon is like a period at the end of a sentence. It means that this command is over and it is time to move to the next line in the source code.

Java Grammar Rule #4: Make Comments

What good would a language be without people being able to talk to each other about what they are doing? **Comments** are the way programmers talk to each other about their source code.

Comments are used to let other programmers know how and why code is written the way it is written. When writing hundreds of lines of source code, programmers can forget why and how they did something. Comments can help a programmer remember how something is intended to work.

Comments are marked by the symbols **//** or **/***.

//   Comment marker used when the comment appears on a single line.

/*   Comment marker used to allow you to write comments that run many lines. When you are ready to stop commenting, you end the comment with the following symbol: */

There are two kinds of comments, **TODO** comments and **EXPLANATORY** comments.

TODO comments explain what needs to be finished at a later time. TODO comments are like notes left by your parents telling you to clean your room or do the dishes.

EXPLANATORY comments explain what is happening in different parts of your applet. Explanatory comments allow other programmers to understand how the code was created. Explanatory comments are like notes you leave for your parents telling them where you have gone and exactly what time you expect to be home.

Java Grammar Rule #5: Define and Extend Your Own Classes

It isn't often that you get a chance to define the classes you want to take. In Java you MUST define your classes by naming them. In the "Hello, World Wide Web" sample, you define the class Hello with the simple statement **class Hello**.

You can **extend** or expand your Hello class by using the **extends java.applet.Applet** class. Extending your Hello class really makes it more powerful. The word **extends** gives your applet (Hello) all the strength and power of **java.applet.Applet**.

Java Grammar Rule #6: Use Braces to Mark Blocks of Code

Braces { } are used to define blocks of code. Using braces is like capitalizing the first letter in a sentence and using a period at the end of a sentence. Braces tell you where things start and stop.

Notice Other Bits of the Code

As you examine Java code, keep your eyes open for new words and terms. For example, you may have noticed that the word **public** often appears in a Java method. This instruction allows other parts of the program to use the same class later in the program. In a sense, public gives other parts of the program a license to use the code found in this public method.

Void is a weird instruction at first. It tells the compiler and the program that the method doesn't return a value. In other words, void is like putting Canadian dollars into a change machine in the U.S. You won't get any change back, your Canadian bill is simply returned by the machine as is.

The numbers 50, 25 are important because they define where the words will appear in the browser window. Change the numbers, and your message will move accordingly. Think of these numbers as X and Y coordinates.

Debriefing

Java is like learning a foreign language; you need to learn how the language is written if you are to use it correctly. It isn't hard to read if you know the code. However, like any foreign language, Java is easier to learn if you actually use it! You can listen to your teacher explain how Italians say, "Hello, my name is Appletto" all day long and never learn Italian. Only when you begin to speak Italian will you truly begin to learn *how* to speak Italian. Likewise, you need to practice the Java grammar rules if you are to remember them. For example, the following rules will become second nature, like riding a bicycle or eating pizza, after you start creating Java source code. Remember to:

- Identify the Classes
- Identify Packages of Tools You Can Use
- Create a Method
- Make Comments
- Define and Extend Your Own Classes
- Use Braces to Mark Blocks of Code

In the next few activities you will practice Java — very simply at first, until you start to understand how Java syntax works — to create some new applets.

Take a Test

Review the terms and questions in your online reading guide. Then, go to the Studio-JPlus Web site and take the Chapter 4 test. Use your favorites or bookmark list to access the Studio-JPlus site.

List of Terms

Repeated Words
> Braces
> Bytecodes
> Classes
> Compiling
> Source code

New Words
> Abstract Windowing Toolkit (AWT)
> Comments
>> TODO
>> EXPLANATORY
> Extend
> Methods
> Objects
> Package
> Paint
> Public
> Reusable code
> Void

 **ou Quack Me Up!**

Java classes serve as templates for objects. Classes are like a cookie cutter, and objects are like the cookie created by the cookie cutter. The attributes and behavior of an object are determined by the class used to create the object. We are going to use a special, pre-created class in this activity. It is called the Graphics class. There are many methods in the Graphics class that allow a Java programmer to create lines and shapes in a variety of sizes. You can combine these shapes to create almost anything you can imagine. We are going to combine some of the shapes in the Graphics class to create the Java duck.

O b j e c t i v e s :

- Use Java's Graphics class.
- Create oval and arc shapes.
- Fill shapes with a color.

Step 1:   Start Visual J++. If there are any windows open from a previous session, close them.

Step 2:   Create a new Visual J++ project.

2A: Click on the **File** menu.

2B: Select **New**.

2C: Select **Text File** from the **New** dialog box, **Files** tab as shown in Figure A8.1.

Figure A8.1
New Dialog Box with
Files Tab in View
A – Text File

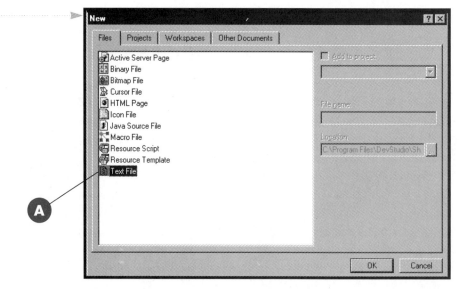

2D: Click **OK**.

2E: Enter the source code in Figure A8.2 into your text editor in Visual J++.

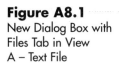

Using Java's Graphics Class

Activity 8

Figure A8.2
Source Code of Java
Duck

```java
import java.awt.Graphics;
import java.awt.Font;
import java.awt.Color;

public class Jduck extends java.applet.Applet
{
    public void paint(Graphics g)
    {
        g.setColor(Color.blue);
        g.drawString("This should look something like a duck.", 2, 9);
        // Drawing the head of the duck
        g.setColor(Color.yellow);
        g.fillOval(50, 10, 60, 100);

        //Drawing the bill of the duck
        g.setColor(Color.orange);
        g.fillOval(27, 65, 100, 50);

        //Drawing the mouth of the duck
        g.setColor(Color.black);
        g.drawArc(45,  65,  65,  30,  0, -180);

        //Drawing the eyes of the duck
        g.fillOval(67, 40, 5, 5);
        g.fillOval(87, 40, 5, 5);
    }
}
```

2F: Select **Save As** from the **File** menu.

2G: Find the Java-?? folder in which you want to save your files.

2H: Enter the name **Jduck.java** in the Name field as shown in Figure A8.3.

Figure A8.3
Save As Dialog Box
A – File name field

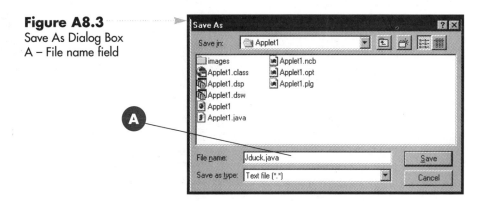

2I: Click **Save**.

2J: Select **Build** from the **Build** menu.

2K: To build source code, you must have an active project workspace. Select **Yes** to the question "Would you like to create a default project workspace?"

2L: If you don't have any errors, select **Execute** from the **Build** menu.

2M: Visual J++ will then ask you to create a **Class file name** for this file. To use the same name you used for **.java** your file, enter **Jduck** in the box underneath the **Class file name** label.

2N: Click **OK**.

2O: You should see the soon-to-be famous Java duck appear before your very eyes!

Debriefing

You have now successfully used the methods supplied in the Graphics class to create a figure. These shapes can be used in a variety of ways to liven up anyone's Web page. The old adage "a picture is worth a thousand words" certainly is true in this case.

Adding Colorful Shapes to Our Java World

Activity 8 introduced you to the Java class called **Graphics**. Now you will use the Graphics class again (along with a few other classes) to create some new shapes, arrange them on the screen in an orderly fashion, and give them some interesting colors. You will also use the **Math** class to generate random numbers. At first glance, it may not be obvious to you why anyone would want to generate a random number. However, there are many occasions when Java programmers find random numbers very useful. For example, there are many types of computer games that rely on the continuous generation of random numbers to determine the behavior of various characters. In your case, you will be using random numbers to decide what color will be used to paint a collection of color boxes.

In addition, you will also gain some experience in creating a Hypertext Markup Language (HTML) document. The strong relationship between HTML and Java is important for you to understand. In fact, Java applets cannot be loaded and executed by Web browsers unless there is a corresponding HTML page available! Watch for this HTML-Java connection as you work your way through the following activity.

O b j e c t i v e s :

- Create a Java project.
- Create a simple HTML document.
- Create a Java applet that displays 12 color boxes on the screen in an orderly fashion.
- Build and execute the Java project.
- Use the Refresh button of the Internet Explorer browser to generate the random colors used to paint the color boxes.

> **Step 1:** Start Visual J++. If there are any windows open from a previous session, close them.

> **Step 2:** Create a new Java project.

> **2A:** Select **New** from the **File** menu.

> **2B:** Click on **Java Project** under the **Projects** tab.

> **2C:** Enter **Colors1** in the **Project name** box. (Make sure you type a capital "C"!)

> **2D:** Click on the Browse button next to the edit box labeled **Location**. Locate your Java-?? folder and click on the **OK** button to select it. Your results should be similar to Figure A9.1.

Figure A9.1
Projects Tab of New
Dialog Box
A – Projects tab
B – Java Project
C – Project name box
D – Location box
E – Browse button (beside
location box)

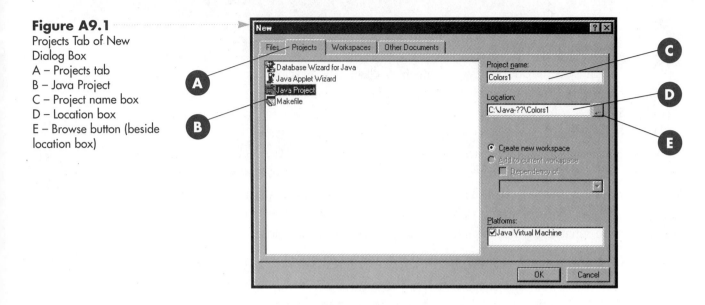

2E: Now click on the **OK** button at the bottom of the **New** dialog box.
Visual J++ will create a new project in your Java-?? folder called
Colors1.

Step 3: Now that your project is created, you need to create a simple HTML document. This document will let the Web browser know that this HTML page
contains a Java applet and will specify the size of the applet on the screen.

3A: Once again, select **New** from the **File** menu.

3B: Click on the **HTML Page** option under the **Files** tab.

3C: Enter **Colors1.html** as the name of the HTML file in the **File name**
box. (Make sure the "C" is capitalized and the **.html** extension is
included!) See Figure A9.2.

Figure A9.2
HTML Page in Files Tab of
New Dialog Box
A – HTML Page option
B – File name box

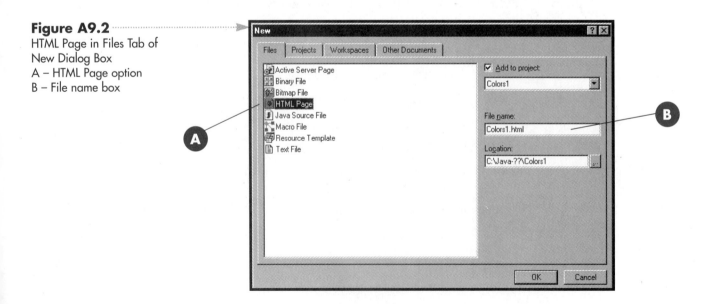

3D: Click on the **OK** button at the bottom of the **New** dialog box. Visual J++ will now create a sample HTML file for you and display it in the right window.

Step 4: Now that your HTML document exists, you will need to make some minor changes to it.

4A: Locate the line of HTML text which reads:

```
<TITLE>Document Title</TITLE>
```

Change the words "Document Title" to "Java Color Boxes: Version 1." The line of HTML text should now read:

```
<TITLE>Java Color Boxes: Version 1</TITLE>
```

4B: Locate the line of HTML text which reads:

```
<!—Insert HTML here —>
```

Replace this line of text with three new lines which read as follows:

```
<APPLET CODE="Colors1.class" WIDTH = 400 HEIGHT = 300>
Java Color Boxes: Version 1
</APPLET>
```

Figure A9.3 shows a complete listing of the entire HTML file as it should now appear.

Figure A9.3
HTML Document after
Changes

```
<HTML>
<HEAD>
<META NAME="GENERATOR" Content="Microsoft Developer Studio">
<META HTTP-EQUIV="Content-Type" content="text/html; charset=iso-8859-1">
<TITLE>Java Color Boxes: Version 1</TITLE>
</HEAD>
<BODY>
<APPLET CODE="Colors1.class" WIDTH = 400 HEIGHT = 300>
Java Color Boxes: Version 1
</APPLET>
</BODY>
</HTML>
```

4C: Check your work carefully. After checking the HTML file, save it by selecting **Save** from the **File** menu.

Step 5: The next step in the applet construction process is to create a new file that will contain your Java source code. This step is done in much the same way you created your HTML file.

5A: Select **New** from the **File** menu.

5B: Click on **Java Source File** under the **Files** tab.

5C: Enter **Colors1.java** as the name of the Java source file in the **File name** box. (Once again, make sure the "C" is capitalized!) See Figure A9.4.

Figure A9.4
Java Source File in Files
Tab of New Dialog Box
A – Java Source File
option
B – File name box

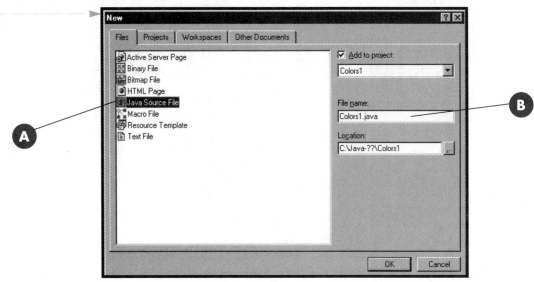

5D: Click on the **OK** button at the bottom of the **New** dialog box. Visual J++ will now create an empty Java source code file.

5E: Enter the following Java source code *exactly* as it appears in Figure A9.5.

Figure A9.5
Java Source Code

```java
import java.applet.*;
import java.awt.*;

public class Colors1 extends Applet
{
    Color BoxColor[];

    public void init()
    {
        int i;
        int red, grn, blu;
        BoxColor = new Color[12];
        for (i = 0; i <= 11; i++)
        {
            red = (int) (Math.random() * 256);
            grn = (int) (Math.random() * 256);
            blu = (int) (Math.random() * 256);
            BoxColor[i] = new Color(red, grn, blu);
        }
        return;
    }
```

(continued)

```
public void paint(Graphics g)
{
    int row, col;
    int x, y;
    y = 25;
    for (row = 0; row <= 2; row++)
    {
        x = 25;
        for (col = 0; col <= 3; col++)
        {
            g.setColor(BoxColor[row*4 + col]);
            g.fillRect(x, y, 50, 50);
            g.setColor(Color.black);
            g.drawRect(x, y, 50, 50);
            x += 100;
        }
        y += 100;
    }
    return;
}

}
```

5F: After you have entered and verified the source code, save it by selecting **Save** from the **File** menu.

Step 6: Now that you have created a Java project, an HTML document, and a Java source code file, the only thing left to do is build the project and execute it.

6A: Build the *Colors1* project by selecting **Build Colors1** from the **Build** menu. If you entered your Java source file correctly, you should see the message "Colors1 - 0 error(s), 0 warning(s)" displayed in the bottom window. If the Visual J++ compiler reports any errors, you will have to find them, correct them, and then repeat Step 6A until all errors are eliminated.

6B: Once your project is completely error free, you may execute the *Colors1* applet by selecting **Execute** from the **Build** menu.

6C: The first time you attempt to execute your applet, Visual J++ will display a dialog box entitled **Information For Running Class**. When this dialog box appears, simply enter **Colors1.class** in the **Class file name** box. Then click **OK**. Visual J++ will automatically tell Internet Explorer to load. When the browser has loaded, it will run your newly created applet.

Step 7: To complete this activity, find the **Refresh** button on the Internet Explorer toolbar. When you click on this button, the browser reloads both the current HTML page and the *Colors1* applet. When the applet executes again, it will randomly pick 12 new colors before it repaints the color boxes. The colors of the 12 boxes will change each time you click on the **Refresh** button in Internet Explorer. Give it a try!

Debriefing

In this activity, you performed several extremely important tasks that Java programmers perform regularly. First, you learned how to create a Java project. Then you learned how to create the HTML document that is responsible for telling the Web browser to load and run your applet. Next you created the actual Java source code which defines the behavior and functionality of your applet. Finally, you learned how to build and execute your applet from within the Visual J++ environment. Well done!

Challenge!

If you want to make sure that you really understand this activity, try changing the Java source code so that it displays colored circles rather than colored squares. (Hint: Try replacing the **fillRect( )** and **drawRect( )** function calls in the **paint( )** method with **fillOval( )** and **drawOval( )** function calls.)

iving Colorful Shapes a Mind of Their Own

One of Java's outstanding features is its ability to support **multi-threaded** applets. Multi-threading may sound like an extremely complicated subject, but our pizza analogy will help make the concept fairly simple to understand. Suppose that you are a very talented pizza maker who works for Senore Appletto. Suppose also that you are only allowed to create a pizza when Senore Appletto calls you on the telephone and explicitly asks you to do so. This could get to be very frustrating, right? Wouldn't you be able to function much better if you were given control of the pizza-making process, and could make a pizza whenever a customer placed an order? This is the idea behind **threads** in Java. If you look closely at the applet you created for Activity 9, you will see that it can only draw its cute little color boxes on the screen whenever the **paint( )** method is called. In this case, the paint( ) method is like a pizza maker, and the Web browser running the applet is like Senore Appletto. It is the Web browser, *not* the applet that decides when the color boxes should be drawn. But in this activity, you are going to change all that. You are going to add some code to your applet which will make it a thread, and it will be able to decide for itself when the color boxes will be displayed.

O b j e c t i v e s :

- Declare a "runnable" Java applet.
- Create a Java thread.
- Generate new random colors at regular intervals.
- Cause the Java "paint" command to occur at regular intervals.

Step 1: Start Visual J++. If there are any windows open from a previous project, close them.

Step 2: Create a new Java project. This process will be the same as it was for Activity 9 except that you will call this project **Colors2** rather than *Colors1*.

2A: Select **New** from the **File** menu.

2B: Click on **Java Project** under the **Projects** tab.

2C: Enter **Colors2** in the **Project name** box. (Make sure you type a capital "C"!)

2D: Click on the Browse button next to the edit box labeled **Location**. Locate your Java-?? folder and click on the **OK** button to select it.

2E: Now click on the **OK** button at the bottom of the **New** dialog box. Visual J++ will create a new project in your Java-?? folder called *Colors2*.

Step 3: Now that your project is created, you will need to create a simple HTML document. This file will be exactly the same as the HTML file you created for Activity 9 except for the name.

3A: Once again select **New** from the **File** menu.

3B: Click on the **HTML Page** option under the **Files** tab.

3C: Enter **Colors2.html** as the name of the HTML file in the **File name** box. (Make sure the "C" is capitalized and the **.html** extension is included!)

3D: Click on the **OK** button at the bottom of the **New** dialog box. Visual J++ will now create a sample HTML file for you and display it in the right window.

Step 4: Now that your HTML document exists, you will need to make some minor changes to it like you did for Activity 9.

4A: Locate the line of HTML text that reads:

```
<TITLE>Document Title</TITLE>
```

Change the words "Document Title" to "Java Color Boxes: Version 2." The line of HTML text should now read:

```
<TITLE>Java Color Boxes: Version 2</TITLE>
```

4B: Locate the line of HTML text that reads:

```
<!--Insert HTML here -->
```

Replace this line of text with three new lines that read as follows:

```
<APPLET CODE="Colors2.class" WIDTH = 400 HEIGHT = 300>
Java Color Boxes: Version 2
</APPLET>
```

Figure A10.1 shows a complete listing of the entire HTML file as it should now appear.

Figure A10.1
HTML Document after
Changes

```
<HTML>
<HEAD>
<META NAME="GENERATOR" Content="Microsoft Developer Studio">
<META HTTP-EQUIV="Content-Type" content="text/html; charset=iso-8859-1">
<TITLE>Java Color Boxes: Version 2</TITLE>
</HEAD>
<BODY>
<APPLET CODE="Colors2.class" WIDTH = 400 HEIGHT = 300>
Java Color Boxes: Version 2
</APPLET>
</BODY>
</HTML>
```

4C: Check your work carefully. After checking the HTML file, save it by selecting **Save** from the **File** menu.

Step 5: The next step in the applet construction process is to create a new file that will contain your Java source code. Once again, this step is done like it was in Activity 9.

5A: Select **New** from the **File** menu.

5B: Click on **Java Source File** under the **Files** tab.

5C: Enter **Colors2.java** as the name of the Java source file in the **File name** box. (Once again, make sure the "C" is capitalized!)

5D: Click the **OK** button at the bottom of the **New** dialog box. Visual J++ will now create an empty Java source code file.

5E: Enter the following Java source code *exactly* as it appears in Figure A10.2.

Figure A10.2
Java Source Code for
Threaded Applet

```java
import java.applet.*;
import java.awt.*;

public class Colors2 extends Applet implements Runnable
{
    Color BoxColor[];
    Thread ColorThread;
    public void init()
    {
        BoxColor = new Color[12];
        return;
    }

    public void start()
    {
        if (ColorThread == null)
        {
            ColorThread = new Thread(this);
            ColorThread.start();
        }
        return;
    }

    public void stop()
    {
        if (ColorThread != null)
        {
            ColorThread.stop();
            ColorThread = null;
        }
    }
}
```

(continued)

```java
public void run()
{
    int i;
    int red, grn, blu;
    while (true)
    {
        for (i = 0; i <= 11; i++)
        {
            red = (int) (Math.random() * 256);
            grn = (int) (Math.random() * 256);
            blu = (int) (Math.random() * 256);
            BoxColor[i] = new Color(red, grn, blu);
        }
        repaint();
        try
        {
            ColorThread.sleep(2000);
        }
        catch (InterruptedException e)
        {
            stop();
            break;
        }
    }
    return;
}

public void paint(Graphics g)
{
    int row, col;
    int x, y;
    y = 25;
    for (row = 0; row <= 2; row++)
    {
        x = 25;
        for (col = 0; col <= 3; col++)
        {
            g.setColor(BoxColor[row*4 + col]);
            g.fillRect(x, y, 50, 50);
            g.setColor(Color.black);
            g.drawRect(x, y, 50, 50);
            x += 100;
        }
        y += 100;
    }
    return;
}
}
```

5F: After you have entered and verified the source code, save it by selecting **Save** from the **File** menu.

Step 6:

Now that you have created a Java project, an HTML document, and a Java source code file, the only thing left to do is build the project and execute it.

6A: Build the *Colors2* project by selecting **Build Colors2** from the **Build** menu. If you entered your Java source file correctly, you should see the message "Colors2 - 0 error(s), 0 warning(s)" displayed in the bottom window. If the Visual J++ compiler reports any errors, you will have to find them, correct them, and then repeat Step 6A until all errors are eliminated.

6B: Once your project is completely error free, you may execute the *Colors2* applet by selecting **Execute** from the **Build** menu.

6C: The first time you attempt to execute your applet, Visual J++ will display a dialog box entitled **Information For Running Class**. When this dialog box appears, simply enter **Colors2.class** in the **Class file name** box. Then click **OK**. Visual J++ will automatically tell Internet Explorer to load. When the browser has loaded, it will run your newly created applet.

Activity 10 is now complete and you should be seeing the results of your effort on the screen. If your applet is running correctly, you should see the 12 color boxes "magically" changing color every two seconds. Let's quickly draw your attention to the parts of your Java source code that make this happen.

First, you told the Java compiler that you wanted this applet to be runnable by adding the words **implements Runnable** to your *Colors2* class definition. Then you declared a thread object called **ColorThread** within your class, and you defined two new methods called **start()** and **stop()** to get the thread started and stopped. Then you added a **run()** method which gives the applet "a mind of its own" by transferring control from the Web browser to the applet. The applet can now decide for itself when the color boxes should be painted by calling the **repaint()** method whenever it feels like it. In this case, it "feels like it" every two seconds because the **run()** method tells the thread to go to sleep for 2000 milliseconds (that's 2 seconds). Then the thread "wakes up," picks 12 new random colors, and tells the applet to paint the color boxes again. Presto! You have just created your first runnable Java applet!

Debriefing

In this activity, you began to explore one of the greatest strengths of the Java programming language — the ability to create threads. Threads are the means by which many Java components are able to take control of their own destiny and act for themselves rather than always responding to requests from an external source. Multi-threaded programming is often thought of as an advanced programming concept, but Java makes it easy to handle. You can now honestly say that you have some actual experience with programming threads. Congratulations!

Challenge!

If you are feeling up to a challenge, try changing the shape of the color boxes to ovals. (Do you remember the names of the Java methods that draw ovals?) You can also experiment with changing the rate at which your new colorful shapes change color. Remember that changing the number that is passed to the **sleep( )** method will cause the colors to change at a different speed. Smaller numbers will make the changes occur faster, while larger numbers will result in a slower rate of change.

aking Your Colorful Shapes Interactive

In Activity 10, you learned how to create a thread that gives an applet control over its own actions. In this activity, you will make it possible for the applet user to affect the behavior of the applet. Let's return to our pizza example for a moment. Giving the pizza maker control over his/her actions is a good first step, but what about the person who is going to *eat* the pizza? Wouldn't it be a good idea to give him/her some input as to how the pizza should be made? In Java terminology, creating an applet that is capable of responding to user input is called making the applet **interactive**. In this activity, you will be adding some code to your color box applet so that it will recognize a mouse click and, if necessary, react to it. Pay close attention to the **mouseDown( )** method that will appear later in the Java source code listing.

O b j e c t i v e s :

- Create an interactive Java applet.
- Create source code that allows the applet to respond to mouse clicks.

Step 1: Start Visual J++. If there are any windows open from a previous project, close them.

Step 2: Create a new Java project. This process will be the same as it was for Activities 9 and 10, except that you will call this project *Colors3*.

    2A: Select **New** from the **File** menu.

    2B: Click on **Java Project** under the **Projects** tab.

    2C: Enter **Colors3** in the **Project name** box. (Make sure you type a capital "C"!)

    2D: Click on the Browse button next to the edit box labeled **Location**. Locate your Java-?? folder and click on the **OK** button to select it.

    2E: Now click on the **OK** button at the bottom of the **New** dialog box. Visual J++ will create a new project in your Java-?? folder called *Colors3*.

Step 3: Now that your project is created, you will need to create a simple HTML document. This file will be exactly the same as the HTML file you created for Activities 9 and 10 except for the name.

    3A: Once again, select **New** from the **File** menu.

    3B: Click on the **HTML Page** option under the **Files** tab.

    3C: Enter **Colors3.html** as the name of the HTML file in the **File name** box. (Make sure the "C" is capitalized and the **.html** extension is included!)

3D: Click on the **OK** button at the bottom of the **New** dialog box. Visual J++ will now create a sample HTML file for you and display it in the right window.

Step 4: Now that your HTML document exists, you will need to make some minor changes to it like you did for Activities 9 and 10.

4A: Locate the line of HTML text that reads:

```
<TITLE>Document Title</TITLE>
```

Change the words "Document Title" to "Java Color Boxes: Version 3." The line of HTML text should now read:

```
<TITLE>Java Color Boxes: Version 3</TITLE>
```

4B: Locate the line of HTML text that reads:

```
<!-Insert HTML here ->
```

Replace this line of text with three new lines that read as follows:

```
<APPLET CODE="Colors3.class" WIDTH = 400 HEIGHT = 300>

Java Color Boxes: Version 3

</APPLET>
```

Figure A11.1 shows a complete listing of the entire HTML file as it should now appear.

Figure A11.1
HTML Document after Changes

```
<HTML>
<HEAD>
<META NAME="GENERATOR" Content="Microsoft Developer Studio">
<META HTTP-EQUIV="Content-Type" content="text/html; charset=iso-8859-1">
<TITLE>Java Color Boxes: Version 3</TITLE>
</HEAD>
<BODY>
<APPLET CODE="Colors3.class" WIDTH = 400 HEIGHT = 300>
Java Color Boxes: Version 3
</APPLET>
</BODY>
</HTML>
```

4C: Check your work carefully. After checking the HTML file, save it by selecting **Save** from the **File** menu.

Step 5: The next step in the applet construction process is to create a new file that will contain your Java source code. Once again, this step is done like it was in Activities 9 and 10.

5A: Select **New** from the **File** menu.

5B: Click on **Java Source File** under the **Files** tab.

5C: Enter **Colors3.java** as the name of the Java source file in the **File name** box. (Once again, make sure the "C" is capitalized!)

5D: Click the **OK** button at the bottom of the **New** dialog box. Visual J++ will now create an empty Java source code file.

5E: Enter the following Java source code *exactly* as it appears in Figure A11.2.

Figure A11.2
Java Source Code for
Interactive Applet

```java
import java.applet.*;
import java.awt.*;

public class Colors3 extends Applet implements Runnable
{
    Color BoxColor[];
    Thread ColorThread;
    public void init()
    {
        BoxColor = new Color[12];
        return;
    }

    public void start()
    {
        if (ColorThread == null)
        {
            ColorThread = new Thread(this);
            ColorThread.start();
        }
        return;
    }

    public void stop()
    {
        if (ColorThread != null)
        {
            ColorThread.stop();
            ColorThread = null;
        }
    }
    public void run()
    {
        int i;
        int red, grn, blu;
        while (true)
        {
            for (i = 0; i <= 11; i++)
            {
                red = (int) (Math.random() * 256);
```

(continued)

```
                        grn = (int) (Math.random() * 256);
                        blu = (int) (Math.random() * 256);
                        BoxColor[i] = new Color(red, grn, blu);
                    }
                    repaint();
                    try
                    {
                        ColorThread.sleep(8000);
                    }
                    catch (InterruptedException e)
                    {
                        stop();
                        break;
                    }
                }
                return;
            }

    public boolean mouseDown(Event evt, int x, int y)
    {
        int index;
        int red, grn, blu;
        index = -1;
        if ((x >  25) && (x <  75) && (y >  25) && (y <  75)) index = 0;
        if ((x > 125) && (x < 175) && (y >  25) && (y <  75)) index = 1;
        if ((x > 225) && (x < 275) && (y >  25) && (y <  75)) index = 2;
        if ((x > 325) && (x < 375) && (y >  25) && (y <  75)) index = 3;
        if ((x >  25) && (x <  75) && (y > 125) && (y < 175)) index = 4;
        if ((x > 125) && (x < 175) && (y > 125) && (y < 175)) index = 5;
        if ((x > 225) && (x < 275) && (y > 125) && (y < 175)) index = 6;
        if ((x > 325) && (x < 375) && (y > 125) && (y < 175)) index = 7;
        if ((x >  25) && (x <  75) && (y > 225) && (y < 275)) index = 8;
        if ((x > 125) && (x < 175) && (y > 225) && (y < 275)) index = 9;
        if ((x > 225) && (x < 275) && (y > 225) && (y < 275)) index = 10;
        if ((x > 325) && (x < 375) && (y > 225) && (y < 275)) index = 11;
        if (index >= 0)
        {
            red = (int) (Math.random() * 256);
            grn = (int) (Math.random() * 256);
            blu = (int) (Math.random() * 256);
            BoxColor[index] = new Color(red, grn, blu);
            repaint();
        }
        return true;
    }
    public void paint(Graphics g)
    {
        int row, col;
        int x, y;
        y = 25;
```

```
        for (row = 0; row <= 2; row++)
        {
            x = 25;
            for (col = 0; col <= 3; col++)
            {
                g.setColor(BoxColor[row*4 + col]);
                g.fillRect(x, y, 50, 50);
                g.setColor(Color.black);
                g.drawRect(x, y, 50, 50);
                x += 100;
            }
            y += 100;
        }
        return;
    }
}
```

5F: After you have entered and verified the source code, save it by selecting **Save** from the **File** menu.

Step 6: Now that you have created a Java project, an HTML document, and a Java source code file, the only thing left to do is build the project and execute it.

6A: Build the *Colors3* project by selecting **Build Colors3** from the **Build** menu. If you entered your Java source file correctly, you should see the message "Colors3 - 0 error(s), 0 warning(s)" displayed in the bottom window. If the Visual J++ compiler reports any errors, you will have to find them, correct them, and then repeat Step 6A until all errors are eliminated.

6B: Once your project is completely error free, you may execute the *Colors3* applet by selecting **Execute** from the **Build** menu.

6C: The first time you attempt to execute your applet, Visual J++ will display a dialog box entitled **Information For Running Class**. When this dialog box appears, simply enter **Colors3.class** in the **Class file name** box. Then click **OK**. Visual J++ will automatically tell Internet Explorer to load. When the browser has loaded, it will run your newly created applet.

Now that you have completed Activity 11, you should see it running on your screen in much the same way that Activity 10 ran. There are two things that are different, however. First, the little squares do not change color by themselves as quickly as they did in Activity 10. In fact, they only change color once every 8 seconds, instead of every 2 seconds. This is because we changed the parameter of the **sleep()** method from 2000 to 8000. The second difference is that you may now click on any one of the 12 color boxes with your mouse pointer and the box will change colors instantly! In other words, the applet itself will change the color of all 12 color boxes every 8 seconds, but you can change the color of any single square as fast as you can click the mouse button. Now we're talking about some very hot stuff!

Debriefing

After completing Activity 11, you have definitely moved much closer to the realm of professional Java coders. Just think for a moment, how useful could a Java applet really be if the user could not interact with it? Although it is true that a noninteractive applet can do some interesting or entertaining things, it can *never* adapt itself to the needs of a particular user unless that user can provide it with input in some way. How popular would a pizza maker be if he/she could not (or perhaps *would* not) interact with his/her pizza-eating customers?

Challenge!

As with Activities 9 and 10, experiment with altering the applet by changing the shape of its color objects or by changing the **sleep()** method parameter.

et Acquainted with Images along the Yellow Brick Road

Using the methods in the Java **Graphics** class to draw rectangles, ovals, arcs, etc., can go a long way toward adding some color and life to a static Web page. However, there are many programming situations where using the graphics class methods simply will not suffice. For example, suppose you wanted to create a Java applet that will display an image of a pizza. You could draw a large yellow circle to represent the crust of the pizza and you could draw a slightly smaller red circle to simulate the pizza sauce. Then you could draw a number of small brown circles to represent pepperoni slices, and maybe a few other shapes to depict pieces of sausage, olives, pineapple chunks, etc. But when you are finished, is your final drawing going to look much like a real pizza? Not hardly. In fact, it would take a considerable amount of effort to render an image that could even be recognized as a pizza. So how do professional Java programmers handle situations like this? Easy. They let professional graphic artists do all the hard work involved in creating photo-realistic images, and then they use the powerful methods in Java's **Image** class to display those images on the screen. You will see how this is accomplished in the following coding activity. Let's pretend we are about to embark on a journey down the Yellow Brick Road, and we would like to display some images of the animals we just might meet along the way.

O b j e c t i v e s :

- Learn to declare and use Java **Image** objects.
- Use **Image** class methods to load and display graphic images.
- Learn to place text labels on graphic images.

Step 1: Start Visual J++. If there are any windows open from a previous session, close them.

Step 2: Create a new Java project. This process will be the same as it was for Activities 9 through 11, except that you will call this project *OhMy*.

2A: Select **New** from the **File** menu.

2B: Click on **Java Project** under the **Projects** tab.

2C: Enter **OhMy** in the **Project name** box. (Make sure you type a capital "O" and a capital "M"!)

2D: Click on the Browse button next to the edit box labeled **Location**. Locate your Java-?? folder and click on the **OK** button to select it.

2E: Now click on the **OK** button at the bottom of the **New** dialog box. Visual J++ will create a new project in your Java-?? folder called *OhMy*.

Step 3: Now that your project is created, you will need to create a simple HTML document. This file will be exactly the same as the HTML file you created for Activities 9 through 11 except for the name.

3A: Once again select **New** from the **File** menu.

3B: Click on the **HTML Page** option under the **Files** tab.

3C: Enter **OhMy.html** as the name of the HTML file in the **File name** box. (Make sure the "O" and "M" are capitalized and the **.html** extension is included!)

3D: Click on the **OK** button at the bottom of the **New** dialog box. Visual J++ will now create a sample HTML file for you and display it in the right window.

Step 4: Now that your HTML document exists, you will need to make some minor changes to it like you did for Activities 9 through 11.

4A: Locate the line of HTML text that reads:

```
<TITLE>Document Title</TITLE>
```

Change the words "Document Title" to "Lions, Tigers, and Bears." The line of HTML text should now read:

```
<TITLE>Lions, Tigers, and Bears</TITLE>
```

4B: Locate the line of HTML text that reads:

```
<!–Insert HTML here –>
```

Replace this line of text with three new lines that read as follows:

```
<APPLET CODE="OhMy.class" WIDTH=400 HEIGHT=300>

Lions, Tigers, and Bears

</APPLET>
```

Figure A12.1 shows a complete listing of the entire HTML file as it should now appear.

Figure A12.1
HTML Document after Changes

```
<HTML>
<HEAD>
<META NAME="GENERATOR" Content="Microsoft Developer Studio">
<META HTTP-EQUIV="Content-Type" content="text/html; charset=iso-8859-1">
<TITLE>Lions, Tigers, and Bears</TITLE>
</HEAD>
<BODY>
<APPLET CODE="OhMy.class" WIDTH=400 HEIGHT=300>
Lions, Tigers, and Bears
</APPLET>
</BODY>
</HTML>
```

4C: Check your work carefully. After checking the HTML file, save it by selecting **Save** from the **File** menu.

Step 5: The next step in the applet construction process is to create a new file which will contain your Java source code. Once again, this step is done like it was in Activities 9 through 11.

5A: Select **New** from the **File** menu.

5B: Click on **Java Source File** under the **Files** tab.

5C: Enter **OhMy.java** as the name of the Java source file in the **File name** box. (Once again, make sure the "O" and "M" are capitalized!)

5D: Click the **OK** button at the bottom of the **New** dialog box. Visual J++ will now create an empty Java source code file.

5E: Enter the following Java source code *exactly* as it appears in Figure A12.2.

Figure A12.2
Java Source Code

```java
import java.applet.*;
import java.awt.*;

public class OhMy extends Applet implements Runnable
{
    int ImageCode;
    Image LionImage;
    Image TigerImage;
    Image BearImage;
    Thread OhMyThread;
    public void init()
    {
        LionImage = createImage(300, 200);
        TigerImage = createImage(300, 200);
        BearImage = createImage(300, 200);
        return;
    }

    public void start()
    {
        if (OhMyThread == null)
        {
            OhMyThread = new Thread(this);
            OhMyThread.start();
        }
        return;
    }
    public void stop()
    {
```

(continued)

```
        if (OhMyThread != null)
        {
            OhMyThread.stop();
            OhMyThread = null;
        }
        return;
    }

public void run()
{
    ImageCode = 0;
    repaint();
    loadImage(LionImage,  "images/lion.jpg");
    loadImage(TigerImage,  "images/tiger.jpg");
    loadImage(BearImage,  "images/bear.jpg");
    while (true)
    {
        ImageCode = 1;
        repaint();
        pause(2500);
        ImageCode = 2;
        repaint();
        pause(2500);
        ImageCode = 3;
        repaint();
        pause(2500);
        ImageCode = 4;
        repaint();
        pause(2500);
    }
}

public void update(Graphics g)
{
    paint(g);
    return;
}

public void paint(Graphics g)
{
    Font text;
    g.setColor(Color.black);
    g.fillRect(0, 0, 400, 300);
    if (ImageCode == 0)
    {
        text = new Font("Ariel", Font.PLAIN, 12);
        g.setFont(text);
        g.setColor(Color.white);
        g.drawString("Loading images...", 50, 50);
    }
```

```
            if (ImageCode == 1)
            {
                g.drawImage(LionImage, 50, 50, this);
                text = new Font("Ariel", Font.BOLD, 24);
                g.setFont(text);
                g.setColor(Color.red);
                g.drawString("LIONS...", 150, 250);
            }
            if (ImageCode == 2)
            {
                g.drawImage(TigerImage, 50, 50, this);
                text = new Font("Ariel", Font.BOLD, 24);
                g.setFont(text);
                g.setColor(Color.green);
                g.drawString("TIGERS...", 150, 250);
            }
            if (ImageCode == 3)
            {
                g.drawImage(BearImage, 50, 50, this);
                text = new Font("Ariel", Font.BOLD, 24);
                g.setFont(text);
                g.setColor(Color.blue);
                g.drawString("BEARS...", 150, 250);
            }
            if (ImageCode == 4)
            {
                text = new Font("Ariel", Font.BOLD, 48);
                g.setFont(text);
                g.setColor(Color.white);
                g.drawString("OH MY!", 110, 160);
            }
            return;
        }

    private void loadImage(Image image, String file)
    {
        boolean done;
        Graphics g;
        Image img;
        img = getImage(getCodeBase(), file);
        g = image.getGraphics();
        while (true)
        {
            done = g.drawImage(img, 0, 0, 300, 200, this);
            if (done) break;
            pause(100);
        }
        return;
    }
```

(continued)

```
    private void pause(long ms)
    {
        try
        {
            OhMyThread.sleep(ms);
        }
        catch (InterruptedException ie)
        {
            OhMyThread.stop();
        }
        return;
    }
}
```

5F: After you have entered and verified the source code, save it by selecting **Save** from the **File** menu.

Step 6: At this point you might expect to compile and run your program as you did in Activities 9 through 11, but this activity is a little different. You need to create a new folder for your lion, tiger, and bear images.

6A: Locate and execute the Windows 95 utility called *Windows Explorer*. This is done by clicking on the Windows 95 **Start** button, positioning your cursor over the **Programs** menu, and then selecting the **Windows Explorer** menu item.

6B: When Windows Explorer comes up, navigate the directory tree on the left until you have found and highlighted your *c:\Java-??\OhMy* project folder. Your *OhMy* project files should be listed on the right.

6C: Create a new folder by selecting the **File** menu, the **New** submenu, and the **Folder** menu item. Enter **images** as the name of your new folder.

6D: Click the Close button for the Windows Explorer program.

Step 7: Download the appropriate image files from the Studio JPlus Web site.

7A: Log onto the Internet using your favorite Web browser (Microsoft Internet Explorer, Netscape Navigator, etc.) Use your Web browser to access the Web page at the following URL:

http://www.studio-jplus.com/appletto.html

7B: Find the hyperlink that refers you to the Java activity images and click on it. This link will take you to a page containing detailed instructions on how to download images to your local hard drive. Follow these instructions carefully and download the three graphic files called

lion.jpg, **tiger.jpg**, and **bear.jpg** to your *Java-??\OhMy\images* folder. You must be certain these files are saved to the proper location or the Java applet for this activity will not function correctly.

Step 8: Now that you have created a Java project, an HTML document, and a Java source code file, and downloaded the necessary images from the Web, the only thing left to do is build the project and execute it.

8A: Build the *OhMy* project by selecting **Build OhMy** from the **Build** menu. If you entered your Java source file correctly, you should see the message "OhMy - 0 error(s), 0 warning(s)" displayed in the bottom window. If the Visual J++ compiler reports any errors, you will have to find them, correct them, and then repeat Step 8A until all errors are eliminated.

8B: Once your project is completely error free, you may execute the *OhMy* applet by selecting **Execute** from the **Build** menu.

8C: The first time you attempt to execute your applet, Visual J++ will display a dialog box entitled **Information For Running Class**. When this dialog box appears, simply enter **OhMy.class** in the **Class file name** box. Then click **OK**. Visual J++ will automatically tell Internet Explorer to load. When the browser is loaded, it will run your newly created applet.

Assuming you have entered, compiled, and executed your Java program correctly, you should be seeing the lion, tiger and bear images on the screen. The program pauses for 2500 milliseconds (that's $2^1/_2$ seconds) between each image, so the entire cycle, including the "OH MY!" message, should take exactly 10 seconds to complete. At this point you should really begin to appreciate the power and convenience of the Java **Image** class. If you don't understand why this is such an important feature to Java programmers, just try drawing a picture of a lion (or tiger or bear) using only the Java **Graphics** class. How many lines of Java code do you think it would take to draw a photo-realistic animal using nothing but rectangles, ovals, and arcs? How many different colors do you suppose you would have to use to make your image look lifelike? Now you get the point, right? So much for the Java duck!

Debriefing

In this activity, you learned the importance of the Java **Image** class and its associated methods. It gives you the power to quickly add high-quality graphic images to your Java applets with minimal effort. Photo-realistic images can do a great deal to enhance the overall quality of an applet and make it a real eye catcher. You should be able to see where the use of high-quality graphics is often more appealing than trying to construct an image on your own with the Java drawing primitives.

Challenge!

If you want to make sure that you have a solid understanding of the Java **Image** class, try changing the appearance of the *OhMy* applet. For instance, you could change the size of the images so that they complete fill the applet window, rather than leaving a black border around its edges. You might also try increasing the total size of the applet window in order to display all three images at once.

Applets on the Superhighway

Creating an applet in Java is only half of the recipe. Once you have a great applet, you need to create a Web page to put it in!

Remember Appletto's pizza box? That box is important to your Java applet. Just like a pizza box protects pizza and keeps it warm, an HTML Web page contains <APPLET> tags that tell your browser all about the Java applet you have inserted into the Web page.

In this sector you will learn how HTML (Hypertext Markup Language) and Java work together to create sizzling Web pages. The Java applet-making skills you learned in Sector 2 will be taken to the next step, as your applets make their way to the World Wide Web.

Sector 3

In Chapter ⑤ *Building Web Pages with Java Applets* will show you how to utilize the Java skills you have learned to create your own Web page. After all, that's why most of us want to learn Java anyway. There are five activities in this section that will help you create your own applet-based Web page. The concepts in each of these activities build upon the previous activities. Therefore, you will have a better picture of the entire process if you complete these activities in order.

Chapter 5

Building Web Pages with Java Applets

In Chapter 1, Senore Appletto explained how applets work on the Web. Do you remember? (If you don't, that's okay. Senore Appletto can't remember where he put his pizza cutter most of the time either. To be perfectly honest, Appletto is one topping short of a supreme pizza.) To review quickly, applets ride the Web like pizza rides in pizza boxes. Applets are placed inside HTML tags for shipment and protection. When a Web browser reads the HTML tags and finds the <APPLET> tag, it knows to download the applet, translate the bytecodes, and run the applet in your browser window.

Nothing could be easier! You are probably thinking to yourself, "Yeah, right. And brain surgery is a minor operation." Never mind. In the next few activities, you will learn that the process of merging applets and HTML Web pages is fairly easy.

The next few activities will walk you through the steps of creating Web pages with applets. Complete the steps for each activity. Then use the Challenge section at the end of the activity to modify the applet.

O b j e c t i v e s :

- Describe the client/server relationship.
- Describe the differences between an Intranet and the Internet.
- Build Web pages using HTML and Java.
- Insert Java applets into Web pages.
- Upload HTML files and applet files with File Transfer Protocol.

Getting the Big Picture

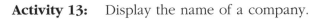

Let's take a quick look at the activities for this sector. Knowing where you are going will help you understand the content of this chapter. You should complete these activities in order, since each one builds on the previous activity's concepts.

Activity 13: Display the name of a company.

Activity 14: Display an image on your Web page. In this case, display a pizza. (What else?)

Activity 15: Create a tickertape or moving announcement that scrolls across the screen.

Activity 16: Add radio buttons, checkboxes, and command buttons to make your applet interactive. These controls will be used to take pizza orders.

Activity 17: Use animation techniques to make Senore Appletto's pizza delivery truck move across the screen.

The Client/Server Relationship

The World Wide Web consists of millions of servers and many millions of clients. However, there is a big difference between what clients and servers do.

A **client** is any device that requests services from a server. Internet clients generally consist of PCs connected to the Internet. A **server** is a computer that generally has more processing power, RAM, and disk storage than the clients connected to it. The task of the server, as the name implies, is to service requests made by clients. As a user on the Web, you can request services from any server as long as you know its address. Once your client PC makes contact with a server, the server can store data, process data, and send data back to you. When you ask for data from a server you are said to be making a **request**.

Web servers are configured to communicate with other computers on the Web. The configuration process uses various protocols. A **protocol** is a set of rules that allow different types of computers to communicate with each other. The most widely used protocol on the Internet is called **TCP/IP** which stands for Transmission Control Protocol/Internet Protocol. As a result of these protocols, most clients on the World Wide Web can communicate with each other through the servers.

How HTML Works With the <APPLET> Tag

A Web server can store Web pages and Java files for access by clients. To create a Web page that a server can deliver over the Web, you must use another important Internet protocol called **HTTP** or **Hypertext Transfer Protocol**. HTTP defines how **HTML (Hypertext Markup Language)** documents are sent and received by computers.

HTML consists of tags. Tags instruct a Web browser how to display the information in the HTML file. Each of these HTML tags has a different purpose and can be combined to produce the desired Web page.

Some of the tags are required with every Web page. These tags identify the Web page to the browser and instruct it how and where to display text, applets, pictures, and other information. The five essential tags for applets appear in the following general order:

```
<HTML>
<HEAD><TITLE></TITLE></HEAD>
<BODY>
<APPLET></APPLET>
</BODY>
</HTML>
```

For most HTML tags, there is a beginning tag, which marks the beginning of a particular section of the Web page, and an ending tag, which marks the end of that section. The ending tags look like their beginning counterparts with a forward slash in front of the tag. For example, the tag <BODY> marks the beginning of the body of the Web page and </BODY> marks the end of the body of the Web page.

A typical set of HTML tags for use with an applet can be seen in Figure 5.1.

Figure 5.1
Basic HTML Tags Needed
to Run a Java Applet

As you can see in Figure 5.1, additional HTML tags can be used to spice up a Web page. For example, <hr> creates a horizontal line and <a href=> </a> creates a hyperlink. Also, notice that HTML can be written in uppercase <HTML> or lowercase </html> letters. HTML, unlike Java, doesn't care about the case of the letters you type.

 //Comment: Remember that Java is very case sensitive.

How the <APPLET> Tag is Organized

If you wish to include a Java applet in your Web page, you must include the <APPLET> tag in your HTML code. The area between the beginning <APPLET> tag and the ending </APPLET> tag is where Java applet information must be placed. (See Figure 5.1.)

Several attributes are available with the applet tag that help you determine the way your applet is displayed. The **CODE** attribute indicates the class file that contains the Java applet to be used with this HTML file. The **WIDTH** and **HEIGHT** attributes define the size of the window Java will have to operate within. The WIDTH and HEIGHT attributes are required.

 //Comment: You can also include some text in the applet area that will be displayed if a user does not have a Java-enabled Web browser. This book, however, assumes that you are using a Java-enabled Web browser.

How to Test Your Applet on an Intranet

As is the case with any software program, you will want to test your applet in a test environment prior to posting the HTML file with its associated Java applet on the World Wide Web. Posting an untested Java applet on the Web allows anyone to view the bugs in your applet or associated HTML file.

The best place to test your applet is in the privacy of your own intranet. An **intranet** describes a network of computers that provide Net-like computing services for a single entity, like a business or school. You can simulate an intranet on your hard drive. To test your applet in a test environment:

1. Save your applet and HTML files in one area (folder or directory) of your hard drive.
2. Open your Web browser.
3. Access the file from your Web browser by selecting **Open** from the **File** menu. (See Figure 5.2.)

Figure 5.2
Select Open from the File Menu

4.   In the text field that is provided, browse for or key the name of your HTML file. (See Figure 5.3.)

Figure 5.3
Browse the Name of
Your HTML File

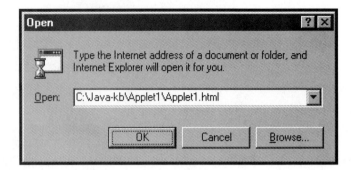

5.   If you have correctly included the applet tag into your HTML file, the HTML file will automatically call your Java file and run it.

After you have thoroughly tested your HTML page and the associated Java applet, you are ready to post your Web page to a Web server.

How to Upload to a Server

In order for your Web page to function correctly, you must copy your HTML file and your Java class files to your Web server.   The most common means of transferring files is with a utility called **FTP**. FTP stands for **File Transfer Protocol.** FTP was designed especially for moving files across the Internet. To use it, you must have an FTP program or client. Windows has a simple FTP client located in its operating system.

Perform the following steps to upload a Web page:

1.   Open your Internet connection.
2.   Open your FTP program or client.

 //Comment: To access the Windows FTP client, select **Run** from the **File** menu. Key **FTP** into the text field of the dialog box as shown in Figure 5.4.

Figure 5.4
Entering FTP into the
Run Dialog box

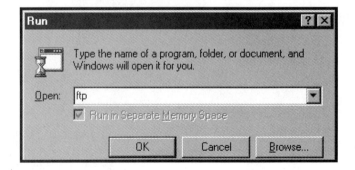

FAQs

What is the difference between the Internet and an intranet?

he Internet consists of millions of servers connected together by TCP/IP and other protocols like the Web's HTTP protocol. Intranets are closed systems that use the same Internet technologies and protocols, but are not available to everyone on the Internet. In other words, intranets are like small, private Internets. The thing to remember is that they both use the same technologies to accomplish similar tasks, but intranets are not open to the public.

The remaining steps in this section assume the use of the Windows FTP client. If you are using another FTP program, the exact steps will vary, so learn to use your specific FTP client.

3. After the FTP program is running, you must indicate the Web server you want to access. This is generally accomplished by selecting the **Open** command followed by the name of the server, as shown in Figure 5.5.

Figure 5.5
The Open FTP Command with Server Name

4. FTP can be a bit confusing. However, if you type the **Help** command and press **Enter**, you will be presented with a list of possible commands you can use, as shown in Figure 5.6.

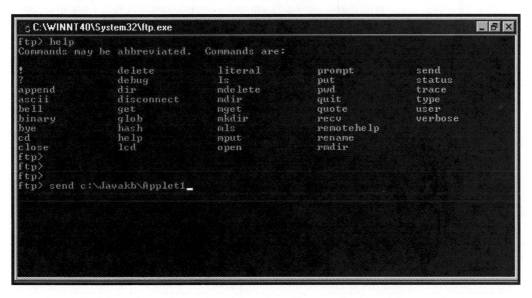

Figure 5.6
Help Will List the FTP Commands You Will Need to Use

5. After you access the desired server, you may have to enter a user name and a password. Once you are logged in, navigate to the directory or folder on the server where you will upload your Web page files.

6. Once you are connected to your server, find the folder or directory you are saving to. This can generally be accomplished by using the **cd** command to change to the desired directory. The **dir** command can also be helpful. The **dir** command lists the directories you are navigating so you can tell where you are in the directory structure of the server.

 //Comment: If you are uploading graphics, you will want to use the binary command. This command will tell FTP to expect pictures and graphics. Using the **binary** mode is a good idea for most file transfers, so enter this command or select this option every time you use FTP unless directed otherwise.

7. Use the **Send** command to upload your files. Specify the path to your Web page files. For example, if your Web page files are located in the c:\msdevstd\projects\appletto directory on your hard drive, you would key the following command using FTP:

send c:\msdevstd\projects\appletto\appletto.html

and

c:\msdevstd\projects\appletto\appletto.class

 //Comment: For another example of how to use the **Send** command, look once again at Figure 5.6. In this illustration, the *Applet1* file is located in the c:\Javakb folder. In each example, the files that are identified are sent or uploaded to the FTP site you have attached to with the Open command.

After loading your Web page files to your Web server, test your pages on the Web to ensure that all the files uploaded properly and everything is functioning correctly. To do so, key the URL (address) of the Web server and then access the correct directory on the server. In our example, we would be searching for the ftp site, **www.myserver.edu** as shown in Figure 5.5. After you upload, the ftp site can often double as a Web site. In our example, the following URL or Web address would be operational:

> ### http://www.myserver.edu

Debriefing

With Visual J++, the software already takes care of much of the work described in this chapter, that is, helping you create and test Web pages. Visual J++ creates a little intranet every time you press the **Build**, **Execute** command. It also creates a minimal HTML file that will run in Internet Explorer. This should make your work even easier as you work with individual applets. However, what if you want to place more than one applet on a

Web page? Then the information in this chapter about adding applet tags and information to an HTML Web page will become very important.

Also, you can't leave your applets on your local hard drive or on a local intranet forever! You will need to use FTP to post your files, including applets and HTML documents, to a Web server capable of being accessed by Web clients. This is the fun part of applet making — sharing your work with the rest of the Web. But before you can share, you must open your FTP software and upload all the needed files to the appropriate Web server.

Now that you know how to test your Web page and then upload it, the following activities will lead you through the development of a Java applet-based Web page. As was mentioned earlier, each activity in this section builds upon the previous activity. The Web page you will have created after Activity 17 will not include all the features that could be included in a Java Web page, but it will include some impressive attributes that can be used to energize any Web page. So without further adieu, let's move to the activities so you can build your own Java applet Web page!

List of Terms

Can you define each of these terms?

Binary
cd
Client
CODE
dir
File Transfer Protocol (FTP)
HEIGHT
Hypertext Markup Language (HTML)
Hypertext Transfer Protocol (HTTP)
Intranet
Protocol
Request
Send
Server
TCP/IP
WIDTH

etting Back to Java Basics

For your first activity in Sector 3, let's suppose that Senore Appletto has decided to start taking pizza orders over the Internet. Suppose also that Senore Appletto has just hired *you* to create his company Web page. Fortunately, by completing the Java activities in Chapter 4, you have gained most of the knowledge and experience you will need to get the job done. You only need to apply that knowledge to this situation, and perhaps adapt it somewhat when necessary. Let's get started by going back to the basics of creating Java applets. If some of the material at the end of Chapter 4 seemed a little complex to you, then this is a great chance to review some very basic concepts. Your first task is simply to display the name of Senore Appletto's pizza company at the top of a Java applet window. Couldn't be easier, right? Let's do it.

O b j e c t i v e s :

- Review the basic structure of a Java applet.
- Review Java variable declarations and assignments.
- Review the Applet class **init( )** method.
- Review the Applet class **paint( )** method.

Step 1: Start Visual J++. If there are any windows open from a previous project, close them.

Step 2: Create a new Java project.

2A: Select **New** from the **File** menu.

2B: Click on **Java Project** under the **Projects** tab.

2C: Enter **Act13** in the **Project name** box.

2D: Click on the browse button next to the edit box labeled **Location**. Locate your Java-?? folder and click on the **OK** button to select it.

2E: Now click on the **OK** button at the bottom of the **New** dialog box. Visual J++ will create a new project in your Java-?? folder called *Act13*.

Step 3: Create an HTML file for this project.

3A: Select the **New** option from the **File** menu.

3B: Click on the **HTML Page** option under the **Files** tab.

3C: Enter **Act13.html** as the name of the HTML file in the **File name** box.

3D: Click on the **OK** button at the bottom of the **New** dialog box. Visual J++ will now create a sample HTML file for you and display it in the right window.

Step 4: Make changes to your HTML file.

4A: Locate the line of HTML text that reads:

```
<TITLE>Document Title</TITLE>
```

Activity **13** Displaying a Company Name

Change the words "Document Title" to "Appletto's Virtual Pizza." The line of HTML text should now read:

```
<TITLE>Appletto's Virtual Pizza</TITLE>
```

4B: Locate the line of HTML text that reads:

```
<!-Insert HTML here ->
```

Replace this line of text with three new lines that read as follows:

```
<APPLET CODE="Act13.class" WIDTH=600 HEIGHT=450>

Appletto's Virtual Pizza

</APPLET>
```

Figure A13.1 shows a complete listing of the entire HTML file as it should now appear.

Figure A13.1
HTML Document after
Changes

```
<HTML>
<HEAD>
<META NAME="Generator" Content="Microsoft Developer Studio">
<META HTTP-EQUIV="Content-Type" content="text/html; charset=iso-8859-1">
<TITLE>Appletto's Virtual Pizza</TITLE>
</HEAD>
<BODY>
<APPLET CODE="Act13.class" WIDTH=600 HEIGHT=450>
Appletto's Virtual Pizza
</APPLET>
</BODY>
</HTML>
```

4C: Check your work carefully. After checking the HTML file, save it by selecting **Save** from the **File** menu.

Step 5: Create your Java applet file.

5A: Select **New** from the **File** menu.

5B: Click on **Java Source File** under the **Files** tab.

5C: Enter **Act13.java** as the name of the Java source file in the **File name** box.

5D: Click on the **OK** button at the bottom of the **New** dialog box. Visual J++ will now create an empty Java source code file.

5E: Enter the following Java code *exactly* as it appears in Figure A13.2.

Figure A13.2
Java Source Code

```
import java.applet.*;
import java.awt.*;

public class Act13 extends Applet
{
    String CompanyName;

    public void init()
    {
        CompanyName = "Appletto's Virtual Pizza";
        return;
    }

    public void paint(Graphics g)
    {
        Font f;

        f = new Font("Ariel", Font.BOLD, 30);
        g.setFont(f);
        g.setColor(Color.blue);
        g.fillRect(0, 0, 600, 450);
        g.setColor(Color.black);
        g.drawRect(0, 0, 599, 449);
        g.setColor(Color.white);
        g.drawString(CompanyName, 135, 50);
        return;
    }

}
```

5F: After you have entered and verified the source code, save it by selecting **Save** from the **File** menu.

Step 6: Build and execute your Java applet.

6A: Build the A*ct13* project by selecting **Build Act13** from the **Build** menu. If you entered the Java source file correctly, you should see the message "Act13 - 0 error(s), 0 warning(s)" displayed in the bottom window. If the Visual J++ compiler reports any errors, you will have to find them, correct them, and then repeat Step 6A until all errors are eliminated.

6B: Once your project is completely error free, execute the *Act13* applet by selecting **Execute** from the **Build** menu.

6C: The first time you attempt to execute your applet, Visual J++ will display a dialog box entitled **Information For Running Class**. When this dialog box appears, simply enter **Act13.class** in the **Class file name** box. Then click **OK**. Visual J++ will automatically tell Internet

Explorer to load. When the browser has loaded, it will run your newly created applet.

If you have coded and compiled this Java program correctly, you should now see version 1 of Appletto's company Web page on the screen. Obviously this applet is very simple, so there is not a lot to explain about it. We simply declare a class variable called **CompanyName** which holds the name of the company we want to display. We initialize the value of that string variable in the **init( )** method, and then we display the string in the **paint( )** method. The company name is displayed in white on a blue background with a black border. What could be easier?

Debriefing

In this activity, you reviewed a few of the most basic Java concepts in order to display the name of Senore Appletto's virtual pizza company. Although this applet may not be very exciting when compared to some of the applets you wrote in Chapter 4, it can be very refreshing to review simple concepts that you understand well. Don't worry, things will definitely start picking up speed very soon. Senore Appletto's company Web page has only just begun.

Challenge!

To make sure you understand the concepts presented in this activity, try changing a few things in the Java source code. For example:

1. Display the name of a different company.
2. Experiment with the colors used to paint the background or the company name.
3. Change the font used for the company name.
4. Change the screen position where the company name is displayed.

Above all, be creative!

Picture Is Worth a Thousand Words

Now that you have a Java applet that displays the name of Senore Appletto's pizza company, it is time to add a distinguishing feature to the Web page. One of the most important things you can do to make a Web page appealing and memorable is to add an appropriate image. Not only can an image convey a great deal of information at a single glance, it can help a page to "stand out from the crowd." Visualize for a moment a page full of advertisements in a newspaper. If you were to place an ad in this paper, what could you do to make your ad catch a potential buyer's attention almost instantly? Obviously you don't want an ad with a lot of words printed in the same boring color as all the other ads, right? What you really want is an eye-catching picture that will immediately tell the customer what you are selling. And then if you have that advertisement printed in a different color (like red or blue rather than black), you are certain to get a much better response from your target audience. Let's apply these ideas to Senore Appletto's Web page. By adding a pizza graphic to your applet, your viewer will know immediately what your Web page is all about. You will also add a little color to the scene in the process.

O b j e c t i v e s :

- Use graphics effectively to improve the appearance of Web pages.
- Review the use of the Java **Image** class.

Step 1: Start Visual J++. If there are any windows open from a previous project, close them.

Step 2: Create a new Java project.

2A: Select **New** from the **File** menu.

2B: Click on **Java Project** under the **Projects** tab.

2C: Enter **Act14** in the **Project name** box.

2D: Click on the browse button next to the edit box labeled **Location**. Locate your Java-?? folder and click on the **OK** button to select it.

2E: Now click on the **OK** button at the bottom of the **New** dialog box. Visual J++ will create a new project in your Java-?? folder called *Act14*.

Step 3: Create an HTML file for this project.

3A: Select the **New** option from the **File** menu.

3B: Click on the **HTML Page** option under the **Files** tab.

3C: Enter **Act14.html** as the name of the HTML file in the **File name** box.

3D: Click on the **OK** button at the bottom of the **New** dialog box. Visual J++ will now create a sample HTML file for you and display it in the right window.

Activity 14 Adding a Graphics Image

Step 4:

Make changes to your HTML file.

4A: Locate the line of HTML text that reads:

```
<TITLE>Document Title</TITLE>
```

Change the words "Document Title" to "Appletto's Virtual Pizza." The line of HTML text should now read:

```
<TITLE>Appletto's Virtual Pizza</TITLE>
```

4B: Locate the line of HTML text that reads:

```
<!—Insert HTML here —>
```

Replace this line of text with three new lines that read as follows:

```
<APPLET CODE="Act14.class" WIDTH=600 HEIGHT=450>
```

```
Appletto's Virtual Pizza
```

```
</APPLET>
```

Figure A14.1 shows a complete listing of the entire HTML file as it should now appear.

Figure A14.1
HTML Document after Changes

```
<HTML>
<HEAD>
<META NAME="Generator" Content="Microsoft Developer Studio">
<META HTTP-EQUIV="Content-Type" content="text/html; charset=iso-8859-1">
<TITLE>Appletto's Virtual Pizza</TITLE>
</HEAD>
<BODY>
<APPLET CODE="Act14.class" WIDTH=600 HEIGHT=450>
Appletto's Virtual Pizza
</APPLET>
</BODY>
</HTML>
```

4C: Check your work carefully. After checking the HTML file, save it by selecting **Save** from the **File** menu.

Step 5:

Create your Java applet file.

5A: Select **New** from the **File** menu.

5B: Click on **Java Source File** under the **Files** tab.

5C: Enter **Act14.java** as the name of the Java source file in the **File name** box.

5D: Click on the **OK** button at the bottom of the **New** dialog box. Visual J++ will now create an empty Java source code file.

5E: Enter the following Java code *exactly* as it appears in Figure A14.2.

```java
import java.applet.*;
import java.awt.*;

public class Act14 extends Applet implements Runnable
{
    boolean PaintFlag;
    String CompanyName;
    Image PizzaImage;
    Thread PizzaThread;

    public void init()
    {
        CompanyName = "Appletto's Virtual Pizza";
        PizzaImage = createImage(400, 200);
        return;
    }

    public void start()
    {
        if (PizzaThread == null)
        {
            PizzaThread = new Thread(this);
            PizzaThread.start();
        }
        return;
    }

    public void stop()
    {
        if (PizzaThread != null)
        {
            PizzaThread.stop();
            PizzaThread = null;
        }
        return;
    }

    public void run()
    {
        PaintFlag = false;
        loadImage(PizzaImage, "images/pizza.gif");
        PaintFlag = true;
        repaint();
        return;
    }

    public void update(Graphics g)
    {
        if (PaintFlag) paint(g);
        return;
    }
```

```java
public void paint(Graphics g)
{
    Font f;

    f = new Font(òArieló, Font.BOLD, 30);
    g.setFont(f);
    g.setColor(Color.blue);
    g.fillRect(0, 0, 600, 450);
    g.setColor(Color.black);
    g.drawRect(0, 0, 599, 449);
    g.setColor(Color.white);
    g.drawString(CompanyName, 135, 50);
    g.drawImage(PizzaImage, 100, 80, this);
    g.setColor(Color.black);
    g.drawRect(100, 80, 399, 199);
    return;
}


private void loadImage(Image image, String file)
{
    boolean done;
    Graphics g;
    Image img;

    img = getImage(getCodeBase(), file);
    g = image.getGraphics();
    while (true)
    {
        done = g.drawImage(img, 0, 0, 400, 200, null);
        if (done) break;
        pause(100);
    }
    return;
}


private void pause(long ms)
{
    try
    {
        PizzaThread.sleep(ms);
    }
    catch (InterruptedException ie)
    {
        PizzaThread.stop();
    }
    return;
}

}
```

5F: After you have entered and verified the source code, save it by selecting **Save** from the **File** menu.

Step 6: Create a new folder called *images* under your current project folder. The complete path of the new folder will be */Java-??/Act14/images*. (If you're not sure how to complete this step, please refer back to Step 6 in Activity 12).

Step 7: Download the graphics image file called **pizza.gif** and save it in the new *images* folder you just created. (Again, if you don't remember exactly how to do this, refer back to Step 7 in Activity 12.)

Step 8: Build and execute your Java applet.

8A: Build the A*ct14* project by selecting **Build Act14** from the **Build** menu. If you entered the Java source file correctly, you should see the message "Act14 - 0 error(s), 0 warning(s)" displayed in the bottom window. If the Visual J++ compiler reports any errors, you will have to find them, correct them, and then repeat Step 8A until all errors are eliminated.

8B: Once your project is completely error free, execute the *Act14* applet by selecting **Execute** from the **Build** menu.

8C: The first time you attempt to execute your applet, Visual J++ will display a dialog box entitled **Information For Running Class**. When this dialog box appears, simply enter **Act14.class** in the **Class file name** box. Then click **OK**. Visual J++ will automatically tell Internet Explorer to load. When the browser has loaded, it will run your newly created applet.

Well, it didn't take long for your Java applet to get a little more complex, did it? Let's quickly review the things we added to your source code to make the pizza image appear. First, we added an **Image** object called **PizzaImage** to allow us to define a graphics image, and then we added a **Thread** object called **PizzaThread** so that we could make the **Act14** applet **Runnable**. We also added the **start( )**, **stop( )**, and **run( )** methods to control the execution of the new thread, and we included two **private** methods called **loadImage( )** and **pause( )** to get the pizza image loaded. Finally, we added a few instructions to the **paint( )** method to actually display the pizza image on the screen. This may seem like a lot of extra code to make a pizza appear, but you can instantly see how the image adds to the value of your Web page, right? In this case, a picture is definitely worth a thousand words!

Debriefing

In this activity, we revisited the topics of threads and images that we previously covered in Chapter 4. The Java **Thread** class gives you the ability to make your applet proactive, and the **Image** class allows you to display photo-quality graphics without having to write pages and pages of Java source code. The value and appeal of Senore Appletto's Web page has been significantly improved because of these enhancements, and you are gaining a lot of valuable experience in the process. What a winning combination!

Challenge!

It is definitely a good idea to cement these concepts in your mind, so try altering various parts of the code to see what happens. Try changing the company name and displaying a different image that would be appropriate for the new business. Experiment with different colors and the position of objects on the screen to see if you can improve the applet's overall appearance. And don't forget to have fun doing it!

aking a Static Web Page Come to Life

Adding an image to Senore Appletto's Web page did a lot to improve its appearance, but now you are going to add something that is equally important—motion. One of the most effective ways to catch a Web surfer's eye is to add some kind of movement to your applet. The two most common ways to add movement are to (1) create an animation, or (2) include a scrolling message, sometimes called a "panning marquee." We will address the issue of animation in Activity 17, but let's take a look at the panning marquee right now. First, you must decide upon an appropriate message to display. Then you will need to add the code to your Java program that will make the message scroll across the screen. To do this, you need to have an active thread controlling the movement of the marquee. Are you ready for this one? Let's get it done!

O b j e c t i v e s :

- Use a Java **Thread** to make a message scroll.
- Make use of the Java **FontMetrics** class.
- Implement double buffering to eliminate display flicker.

Step 1: Start Visual J++. If there are any windows open from a previous project, close them.

Step 2: Create a new Java project.

2A: Select **New** from the **File** menu.

2B: Click on **Java Project** under the **Projects** tab.

2C: Enter **Act15** in the **Project name** box.

2D: Click on the browse button next to the edit box labeled **Location**. Locate your Java-?? folder and click on the **OK** button to select it.

2E: Now click on the **OK** button at the bottom of the **New** dialog box. Visual J++ will create a new project in your Java-?? folder called *Act15*.

Step 3: Create an HTML file for this project.

3A: Select the **New** option from the **File** menu.

3B: Click on the **HTML Page** option under the **Files** tab.

3C: Enter **Act15.html** as the name of the HTML file in the **File name** box.

3D: Click on the **OK** button at the bottom of the **New** dialog box. Visual J++ will now create a sample HTML file for you and display it in the right window.

Activity **15** Adding a Panning Marquee

Make changes to your HTML file.

4A: Locate the line of HTML text that reads:

```
<TITLE>Document Title</TITLE>
```

Change the words "Document Title" to "Appletto's Virtual Pizza." The line of HTML text should now read:

```
<TITLE>Appletto's Virtual Pizza</TITLE>
```

4B: Locate the line of HTML text that reads:

```
<!-Insert HTML here ->
```

Replace this line of text with three new lines that read as follows:

```
<APPLET CODE="Act15.class" WIDTH=600 HEIGHT=450>

Appletto's Virtual Pizza

</APPLET>
```

Figure A15.1 shows a complete listing of the entire HTML file as it should now appear.

Figure A15.1
HTML Document after Changes

```
<HTML>
<HEAD>
<META NAME="Generator" Content="Microsoft Developer Studio">
<META HTTP-EQUIV="Content-Type" content="text/html; charset=iso-8859-1">
<TITLE>Appletto's Virtual Pizza</TITLE>
</HEAD>
<BODY>
<APPLET CODE="Act15.class" WIDTH=600 HEIGHT=450>
Appletto's Virtual Pizza
</APPLET>
</BODY>
</HTML>
```

4C: Check your work carefully. After checking the HTML file, save it by selecting **Save** from the **File** menu.

Step **5:** Create your Java applet file.

5A: Select **New** from the **File** menu.

5B: Click on **Java Source File** under the **Files** tab.

5C: Enter **Act15.java** as the name of the Java source file in the **File name** box.

5D: Click on the **OK** button at the bottom of the **New** dialog box. Visual J++ will now create an empty Java source code file.

5E: Enter the following Java code *exactly* as it appears in Figure A15.2.

```java
import java.applet.*;
import java.awt.*;

public class Act15 extends Applet implements Runnable
{
    boolean PaintFlag;
    String CompanyName;
    Image PizzaImage;
    Thread PizzaThread;
    String MarqueeText;
    int MarqLeft, MarqRght;
    Image BackPage;
    Graphics OffScreen;

    public void init()
    {
        CompanyName = "Appletto's Virtual Pizza";
        MarqueeText = "The best pizza in Cyberspace. Order now!";
        MarqLeft = MarqRght = 0;
        BackPage = createImage(600, 450);
        OffScreen = BackPage.getGraphics();
        return;
    }

    public void start()
    {
        if (PizzaThread == null)
        {
            PizzaThread - new Thread(this);
            PizzaThread.start();
        }
        return;
    }

    public void stop()
    {
        if (PizzaThread != null)
        {
            PizzaThread.stop();
            PizzaThread = null;
        }
        return;
    }

    public void run()
    {   Font f1, f2;
        FontMetrics fm;
        int strlen;

        PaintFlag = false;
        f1 = new Font("Ariel", Font.BOLD, 30);
```

```
                  f2 = new Font("Ariel", Font.ITALIC, 24);
                  fm = getFontMetrics(f2);
                  strlen = fm.stringWidth(MarqueeText);
                  OffScreen.setFont(f1);
                  OffScreen.setColor(Color.blue);
                  OffScreen.fillRect(0, 0, 600, 450);
                  OffScreen.setColor(Color.black);
                  OffScreen.drawRect(0, 0, 599, 449);
                  OffScreen.setColor(Color.white);
                  OffScreen.drawString(CompanyName, 135, 50);
                  loadImage(PizzaImage, "images/pizza.gif");
                  OffScreen.setColor(Color.black);
                  OffScreen.drawRect(100, 80, 399, 199);
                  OffScreen.setFont(f2);
                  PaintFlag = true;
                  while (true)
                  {
                      if (MarqRght <= 0)
                      {
                          MarqLeft = 600;
                          MarqRght = MarqLeft + strlen;
                      }
                      OffScreen.setColor(Color.yellow);
                      OffScreen.fillRect(0, 320, 600, 50);
                      OffScreen.setColor(Color.blue);
                      OffScreen.drawString(MarqueeText, MarqLeft, 352);
                      OffScreen.setColor(Color.black);
                      OffScreen.drawRect(0, 320, 599, 49);
                      repaint();
                      pause(50);
                      MarqLeft -= 3;
                      MarqRght -= 3;
                  }
              }

              public void update(Graphics g)
              {
                  if (PaintFlag) paint(g);
                  return;
              }

              public void paint(Graphics g)
              {
                  g.drawImage(BackPage, 0, 0, this);
                  return;
              }
```

(continued)

Figure A15.2
Java Source Code
[continued]

```java
private void loadImage(Image image, String file)
{
    boolean done;

    image = getImage(getCodeBase(), file);
    while (true)
    {
        done = OffScreen.drawImage(image, 100, 80, 400, 200, null);
        if (done) break;
        pause(100);
    }
    return;
}

private void pause(long ms)
{
    try
    {
        PizzaThread.sleep(ms);
    }
    catch (InterruptedException ie)
    {
        PizzaThread.stop();
    }
    return;
}

}
```

5F: After you have entered and verified the source code, save it by selecting **Save** from the **File** menu.

Step 6: Create a new folder called *images* under your current project folder. The complete path of the new folder will be *Java-??**Act15**images*. (If you're not sure how to complete this step, please refer back to Step 6 in Activity 12.)

Step 7: Download the graphics file called **pizza.gif** and save it in the new *images* folder you just created. (Again, if you don't remember exactly how to do this, refer back to Step 7 of Activity 12.)

Step 8: Build and execute your Java applet.

8A: Build the A*ct15* project by selecting **Build Act15** from the **Build** menu. If you entered the Java source file correctly, you should see the message "Act15 - 0 error(s), 0 warning(s)" displayed in the bottom window. If the Visual J++ compiler reports any errors, you will have to find them, correct them, and then repeat Step 8A until all errors are eliminated.

8B: Once your project is completely error free, execute the *Act15* applet by selecting **Execute** from the **Build** menu.

8C: The first time you attempt to execute your applet, Visual J++ will display a dialog box entitled **Information For Running Class**. When this dialog box appears, simply enter **Act15.class** in the **Class file name** box. Then click **OK**. Visual J++ will automatically tell Internet Explorer to load. When the browser has loaded, it will run your newly created applet.

Now do you see how a little motion can liven up a static Web page? There are several important points that this applet demonstrates, so let's quickly discuss those concepts in terms of the objectives we defined at the beginning of the activity.

First, take note of the **run( )** method. Using this method, the main applet thread (called **PizzaThread**) takes control and paints the various parts of the screen in their initial state. Then the applet enters an "infinite while loop" that is responsible for making the marquee text move. Basically, the thread just paints the yellow rectangle, draws the message at its current location, and outlines the yellow rectangle in black. Then the applet goes to sleep for 50 milliseconds, adjusts the position of the message 3 pixels to the left, and then paints the marquee components again.

Second, you may have noticed in the **run( )** method the appearance of a previously unused Java class called **FontMetrics**. This class gives you the ability to determine the size of **String** objects (that are displayed in a particular font) in terms of screen pixels. We use this class to calculate the point at which the trailing edge of the scrolling Marquee text disappears off the left side of the screen. Then we simply reset its position back to the right side of the screen.

Last but not least, this activity introduces the concept of double buffering, which is an advanced and effective technique for eliminating screen flicker. Notice that the **paint( )** method has become extremely small and simple. In fact, the only thing it does is display an image called **BackPage** on the screen. Where did this image come from? We created it in the **init( )** method with the Java library method called **createImage( )**. We also created a new **Graphics** object called **OffScreen** that gives us all of the same drawing capabilities we would normally have in the **paint( )** method. The difference, however, is that anything we draw using the **OffScreen** graphics object goes onto the **BackPage** image in memory rather than onto the screen. This means that the **run( )** method can now paint several image components without the user seeing anything on the screen. Then when the **repaint( )** method is invoked, the regular **paint( )** method can draw the entire full-screen image in a single, seamless sweep rather than one small piece at a time. Why did you add this extra logic to your applet? Because if you didn't, you would see an annoying flicker on the screen while the panning marquee is painted over and over again. If you want professional-looking results, sometimes you have to take that extra step.

Debriefing

In this activity, you learned that adding movement to an applet can make it stand out and be noticed. In the process, you also learned a few new Java programming techniques that can be applied to a variety of situations. Threads are essential to every Java applet that needs to act within, rather than simply react to, its environment. Font metrics will also prove to be useful whenever knowing the pixel dimensions of characters or text strings is important. And double buffering is an important technique to master whenever you need to implement scrolling text or image animation with professional quality results. Congratulations! You are making tremendous progress.

Challenge!

Perhaps the most valuable concept you can learn from this activity is the importance of using double buffering in applets that implement movement. To give you a greater appreciation for the benefits of double buffering, try rewriting this applet *without* using the off-screen buffer. To do this, simply move all of the graphics functions (like **drawRect( )**, **fillRect( )**, **drawString( )**, etc.) out of the **run( )** method and into the **paint( )** method where you might normally expect to find them. But be prepared to cover your eyes, because the resulting screen flicker is sure to drive you crazy!

 Debug: Make sure all functions you move are placed before the "return" statement in the paint method.

aking Your Java Applet Completely Interactive

Let's briefly review the things you've accomplished for Senore Appletto in the previous three activities. First, you displayed a colorful company name, then you added an eye-catching pizza image, and finally, you included a panning marquee to really spice things up. So whatÔs left to accomplish? You need to make your applet interactive. Applets become interactive when they allow the user to make choices or decisions using the mouse or the keyboard. If you apply this to Senore Appletto's Web page, it should be immediately obvious that so far you have done nothing to allow the user to interact with your applet. You are going to remedy that situation right now.

In this activity, you will be creating a virtual pizza order form so that people from all over the world will be able to order pizza from Senore Appletto. Be forewarned that the Java code for this activity will be much longer than any previous activity, so you may want to refer back to the Preface that explains how to download the code from the Studio J-Plus Web site.

O   b   j   e   c   t   i   v   e   s   :

- Implement a Java method to respond to mouse clicks.
- Implement a Java method to respond to keystrokes.
- Incorporate user-interactive controls into a Java applet.
- Create and use command buttons.
- Create and use text boxes.
- Create and use radio buttons.
- Create and use check boxes.

Step 1: Start Visual J++. If there are any windows open from a previous project, close them.

Step 2: Create a new Java project.

2A: Select **New** from the **File** menu.

2B: Click on **Java Project** under the **Projects** tab.

2C: Enter **Act16** in the **Project name** box.

2D: Click on the browse button next to the edit box labeled **Location**. Locate your Java-?? folder and click on the **OK** button to select it.

2E: Now click on the **OK** button at the bottom of the **New** dialog box. Visual J++ will create a new project in your Java-?? folder called *Act16*.

Step 3: Create an HTML file for this project.

3A: Select the **New** option from the **File** menu.

3B: Click on the **HTML Page** option under the **Files** tab.

3C: Enter **Act16.html** as the name of the HTML file in the **File name** box.

3D: Click on the **OK** button at the bottom of the **New** dialog box. Visual J++ will now create a sample HTML file for you and display it in the right window.

Step 4: Make changes to your HTML file.

4A: Locate the line of HTML text that reads:

```
<TITLE>Document Title</TITLE>
```

Change the words "Document Title" to "Appletto's Virtual Pizza." The line of HTML text should now read:

```
<TITLE>Appletto's Virtual Pizza</TITLE>
```

4B: Locate the line of HTML text that reads:

```
<!—Insert HTML here —>
```

Replace this line of text with three new lines that read as follows:

```
<APPLET CODE="Act16.class" WIDTH=600 HEIGHT=450>

Appletto's Virtual Pizza

</APPLET>
```

Figure A16.1 shows a complete listing of the entire HTML file as it should now appear.

Figure A16.1
HTML Document after Changes

```
<HTML>
<HEAD>
<META NAME="Generator" Content="Microsoft Developer Studio">
<META HTTP-EQUIV="Content-Type" content="text/html; charset=iso-8859-1">
<TITLE>Appletto's Virtual Pizza</TITLE>
</HEAD>
<BODY>
<APPLET CODE="Act16.class" WIDTH=600 HEIGHT=450>
Appletto's Virtual Pizza
</APPLET>
</BODY>
</HTML>
```

4C: Check your work carefully. After checking the HTML file, save it by selecting **Save** from the **File** menu.

Step 5: Create your Java applet file.

5A: Select **New** from the **File** menu.

5B: Click on **Java Source File** under the **Files** tab.

5C: Enter **Act16.java** as the name of the Java source file in the **File name** box.

5D: Click on the **OK** button at the bottom of the **New** dialog box. Visual J++ will now create an empty Java source code file.

5E: Enter the following Java code *exactly* as it appears in Figure A16.2.

Figure A16.2
Java Source Code

```java
import java.applet.*;
import java.awt.*;

public class Act16 extends Applet implements Runnable
{
    final byte ORDERNOW = 11;
    final byte CANCEL = 13;
    final byte NAME = 21;
    final byte ADDRESS = 22;
    final byte PHONE = 23;
    final byte SMALL = 31;
    final byte MEDIUM = 32;
    final byte LARGE = 33;
    final byte PEPPERONI = 41;
    final byte SAUSAGE = 42;
    final byte MUSHROOMS = 43;
    final byte OLIVES = 44;
    final byte PINEAPPLE = 45;
    final byte KEYDOWN = 50;

    boolean PaintFlag;
    String CompanyName;
    Image PizzaImage;
    Thread PizzaThread;
    String MarqueeText;
    int MarqLeft, MarqRght;
    Image BackPage;
    Graphics OffScreen;
    CmndButton OrderNow;
    CmndButton Submit, Cancel;
    TextBox Name, Address, Phone;
    RadioButton Small, Medium, Large;
    CheckBox Pepperoni, Sausage, Mushrooms, Olives, Pineapple;
    byte EventCode;
```

(continued)

```
public void init()
{
    CompanyName = "Appletto's Virtual Pizza";
    MarqueeText = "The best pizza in Cyberspace. Order now!";
    MarqLeft = MarqRght = 0;
    BackPage = createImage(600, 450);
    OffScreen = BackPage.getGraphics();
    OrderNow = new CmndButton(240, 400, "Order Now!");
    Name = new TextBox(100, 90, "Customer Name:");
    Address = new TextBox(100, 115, "Street Address:");
    Phone = new TextBox(100, 140, "Phone Number:");
    Small = new RadioButton(100, 220, "Small");
    Medium = new RadioButton(100, 250, "Medium");
    Large = new RadioButton(100, 280, "Large");
    Pepperoni = new CheckBox(350, 220, "Pepperoni");
    Sausage = new CheckBox(350, 250, "Sausage");
    Mushrooms = new CheckBox(350, 280, "Mushrooms");
    Olives = new CheckBox(350, 310, "Olives");
    Pineapple = new  CheckBox(350, 340, "Pineapple");
    Submit = new CmndButton(150, 400, "  Submit  ");
    Cancel = new CmndButton(330, 400, "  Cancel  ");
    return;
}

public boolean keyDown(Event e, int key)
{
    if (Name.active())
    {
        if (key == 9)
        {
            EventCode = ADDRESS;
            return true;
        }
        Name.process(key);
        EventCode = KEYDOWN;
        return true;
    }
    if (Address.active())
    {
        if (key == 9)
        {
            EventCode = PHONE;
            return true;
        }
        Address.process(key);
        EventCode = KEYDOWN;
        return true;
    }
```

```
                 if (Phone.active())
                 {
                     if (key == 9)
                     {
                         EventCode = NAME;
                         return true;
                     }
                     Phone.process(key);
                     EventCode = KEYDOWN;
                     return true;
                 }
                 return false;
             }

             public boolean mouseDown(Event e, int x, int y)
             {
                 if (OrderNow.clicked(x, y)) EventCode = ORDERNOW;
                 if (Name.clicked(x, y)) EventCode = NAME;
                 if (Address.clicked(x, y)) EventCode = ADDRESS;
                 if (Phone.clicked(x, y)) EventCode = PHONE;
                 if (Small.clicked(x, y)) EventCode = SMALL;
                 if (Medium.clicked(x, y)) EventCode = MEDIUM;
                 if (Large.clicked(x, y)) EventCode = LARGE;
                 if (Pepperoni.clicked(x, y)) EventCode = PEPPERONI;
                 if (Sausage.clicked(x, y)) EventCode = SAUSAGE;
                 if (Mushrooms.clicked(x, y)) EventCode = MUSHROOMS;
                 if (Olives.clicked(x, y)) EventCode = OLIVES;
                 if (Pineapple.clicked(x, y)) EventCode = PINEAPPLE;
                 if (Cancel.clicked(x, y)) EventCode = CANCEL;
                 if (EventCode != 0) return true;
                 return false;
             }

             public void paint(Graphics g)
             {
                 g.drawImage(BackPage, 0, 0, this);
                 return;
             }

             public void run()
             {
                 while (true)
                 {
                     drawIntro();
                     repaint();
                     while (true)
                     {
                         if (EventCode == ORDERNOW)
                         {
                             doCmndButton();
                             break;
                         }
```

(continued)

```
                    drawMarquee();
                    repaint();
                    pause(125);
            }
            drawForm();
            repaint();
            while (true)
            {
                if (EventCode == KEYDOWN) doTextBox();
                if (EventCode == NAME) doTextBox();
                if (EventCode == ADDRESS) doTextBox();
                if (EventCode == PHONE) doTextBox();
                if (EventCode == SMALL) doRadioButton();
                if (EventCode == MEDIUM) doRadioButton();
                if (EventCode == LARGE) doRadioButton();
                if (EventCode == PEPPERONI) doCheckBox();
                if (EventCode == SAUSAGE) doCheckBox();
                if (EventCode == MUSHROOMS) doCheckBox();
                if (EventCode == OLIVES) doCheckBox();
                if (EventCode == PINEAPPLE) doCheckBox();
                if (EventCode == CANCEL)
                {
                    doCmndButton();
                    break;
                }
                pause(125);
            }
        }
    }

    public void start()
    {
        if (PizzaThread == null)
        {
            PizzaThread = new Thread(this);
            PizzaThread.start();
        }
        return;
    }

    public void stop()
    {
        if (PizzaThread != null)
        {
            PizzaThread.stop();
            PizzaThread = null;
        }
        return;
    }
```

```
public void update(Graphics g)
{
    if (PaintFlag) paint(g);
    return;
}

private void loadImage(Image image, String file)
{
    boolean done;

    PaintFlag = false;
    image = getImage(getCodeBase(), file);
    while (true)
    {
        done = OffScreen.drawImage(image, 100, 80, 400, 200, null);
        if (done) break;
        pause(125);
    }
    PaintFlag = true;
    return;
}


private void pause(long ms)
{
    try
    {
        PizzaThread.sleep(ms);
    }
    catch (InterruptedException ie)
    {
        PizzaThread.stop();
    }
    return;
}

private void doCmndButton()
{
    if (EventCode == ORDERNOW)
    {
        OrderNow.push(OffScreen);
        OrderNow.disable();
    }
    if (EventCode == CANCEL)
    {
        Cancel.push(OffScreen);
        Cancel.disable();
    }
    repaint();
    pause(500);
    EventCode = 0;
    return;
}
```

(continued)

```java
    private void doTextBox()
    {
        if (EventCode == NAME)
        {

            Name.toggle(OffScreen);
            Address.clear(OffScreen);
            Phone.clear(OffScreen);
        }
        if (EventCode == ADDRESS)
        {

            Name.clear(OffScreen);
            Address.toggle(OffScreen);
            Phone.clear(OffScreen);
        }
        if (EventCode == PHONE)
        {

            Name.clear(OffScreen);
            Address.clear(OffScreen);
            Phone.toggle(OffScreen);
        }
        if (EventCode == KEYDOWN)
        {

            if (Name.active()) Name.update(OffScreen);
            if (Address.active()) Address.update(OffScreen);
            if (Phone.active()) Phone.update(OffScreen);
        }
        repaint();
        EventCode = 0;
        return;
    }

    private void doRadioButton()
    {
        if (EventCode == SMALL)
        {
            Small.toggle(OffScreen);
            Medium.clear(OffScreen);
            Large.clear(OffScreen);
        }
        if (EventCode == MEDIUM)
        {
            Small.clear(OffScreen);
            Medium.toggle(OffScreen);
            Large.clear(OffScreen);
        }
        if (EventCode == LARGE)
        {
            Small.clear(OffScreen);
            Medium.clear(OffScreen);
            Large.toggle(OffScreen);
        }
        repaint();
        EventCode = 0;
```

```
                    return;
               }

               private void doCheckBox()
               {
                   if (EventCode == PEPPERONI) Pepperoni.toggle(OffScreen);
                   if (EventCode == SAUSAGE) Sausage.toggle(OffScreen);
                   if (EventCode == MUSHROOMS) Mushrooms.toggle(OffScreen);
                   if (EventCode == OLIVES) Olives.toggle(OffScreen);
                   if (EventCode == PINEAPPLE) Pineapple.toggle(OffScreen);
                   repaint();
                   EventCode = 0;
                   return;
               }

               private void drawIntro()
               {
                   OffScreen.setColor(Color.blue);
                   OffScreen.fillRect(0, 0, 600, 450);
                   OffScreen.setColor(Color.black);
                   OffScreen.drawRect(0, 0, 599, 449);
                   OffScreen.setColor(Color.white);
                   OffScreen.setFont(new Font("Arial", Font.BOLD, 30));
                   OffScreen.drawString(CompanyName, 135, 50);
                   loadImage(PizzaImage, "images/pizza.gif");
                   OffScreen.setColor(Color.black);
                   OffScreen.drawRect(100, 80, 399, 199);
                   OrderNow.enable();
                   OrderNow.show(OffScreen);
                   return;
               }

               private void drawMarquee()
               {
                   int strlen;
                   Font f;
                   FontMetrics fm;

                   f = new Font("Arial", Font.ITALIC, 24);
                   fm = getFontMetrics(f);
                   strlen = fm.stringWidth(MarqueeText);
                   if (MarqRght <= 0)
                   {
                       MarqLeft = 600;
                       MarqRght = MarqLeft + strlen;
                   }
                   OffScreen.setColor(Color.yellow);
                   OffScreen.fillRect(0, 320, 600, 50);
                   OffScreen.setColor(Color.blue);
                   OffScreen.setFont(f);
                   OffScreen.drawString(MarqueeText, MarqLeft, 352);
                   OffScreen.setColor(Color.black);
```

(continued)

```
                        OffScreen.drawRect(0, 320, 599, 49);
                        MarqLeft -= 8;
                        MarqRght -= 8;
                        return;
                    }

                private void drawForm()
                    {
                        OffScreen.setColor(Color.white);
                        OffScreen.fillRect(1, 1, 598, 448);
                        OffScreen.setColor(Color.black);
                        OffScreen.setFont(new Font("Arial", Font.BOLD, 30));
                        OffScreen.drawString("Virtual Pizza Order Form", 135, 50);
                        drawFrame("Customer Information", 50, 75, 500, 100);
                        Name.show(OffScreen);
                        Address.show(OffScreen);
                        Phone.show(OffScreen);
                        drawFrame("Pizza Size", 50, 200, 225, 115);
                        Small.show(OffScreen);
                        Medium.show(OffScreen);
                        Large.show(OffScreen);
                        drawFrame("Pizza Toppings", 300, 200, 250, 175);
                        Pepperoni.show(OffScreen);
                        Sausage.show(OffScreen);
                        Mushrooms.show(OffScreen);
                        Olives.show(OffScreen);
                        Pineapple.show(OffScreen);
                        Submit.show(OffScreen);
                        Cancel.enable();
                        Cancel.show(OffScreen);
                        return;
                    }

                private void drawFrame(String s, int x, int y, int w, int h)
                    {
                        int n;
                        Font f;
                        FontMetrics fm;

                        f = new Font("Arial", Font.BOLD, 12);
                        fm = getFontMetrics(f);
                        n = fm.stringWidth(s);
                        OffScreen.setColor(Color.black);
                        OffScreen.drawRect(x, y, w, h);
                        OffScreen.setColor(Color.white);
                        OffScreen.drawLine(x + 10, y, x + n + 14, y);
                        OffScreen.setColor(Color.black);
                        OffScreen.setFont(f);
                        OffScreen.drawString(s, x + 12, y + 4);
                        return;
                    }

            }
```

```
class CmndButton extends Object
{
    boolean Enabled;
    int Left;
    int Top;
    String Label;

    public CmndButton(int x, int y, String lbl)
    {
        Left = x;
        Top = y;
        Label = lbl;
    }

    public boolean clicked(int x, int y)
    {
        if (!Enabled) return false;
        if (x < Left) return false;
        if (x > Left + 119) return false;
        if (y < Top) return false;
        if (y > Top + 29) return false;
        return true;
    }

    public void disable()
    {
        Enabled = false;
        return;
    }

    public void enable()
    {
        Enabled = true;
        return;
    }

    public void push(Graphics g)
    {
        g.setColor(Color.lightGray);
        g.fillRect(Left, Top, 120, 30);
        g.setColor(Color.black);
        g.drawRect(Left - 1, Top - 1, 121, 31);
        g.setColor(Color.gray);
        g.drawLine(Left, Top, Left + 119, Top);
        g.drawLine(Left, Top, Left, Top + 29);
        g.setColor(Color.black);
        g.setFont(new Font("Courier", Font.BOLD, 16));
        g.drawString(Label, Left + 13, Top + 20);
        return;
    }
```

(continued)

```java
public void show(Graphics g)
{
    Color c;

    g.setColor(Color.lightGray);
    g.fillRect(Left, Top, 120, 30);
    g.setColor(Color.black);
    g.drawRect(Left - 1, Top - 1, 121, 31);
    g.setColor(Color.white);
    g.drawLine(Left, Top, Left + 119, Top);
    g.drawLine(Left + 1, Top + 1, Left + 118, Top + 1);
    g.drawLine(Left, Top, Left, Top + 29);
    g.drawLine(Left + 1, Top + 1, Left + 1, Top + 28);
    g.setColor(Color.gray);
    g.drawLine(Left + 1, Top + 29, Left + 119, Top + 29);
    g.drawLine(Left + 2, Top + 28, Left + 118, Top + 28);
    g.drawLine(Left + 119, Top + 1, Left + 119, Top + 29);
    g.drawLine(Left + 118, Top + 2, Left + 118, Top + 28);
    c = (Enabled) ? Color.black : Color.gray;
    g.setColor(c);
    g.setFont(new Font("Courier", Font.BOLD, 16));
    g.drawString(Label, Left + 12, Top + 19);
    return;
    }

}


class TextBox extends Object
{
    boolean Selected;
    int Left;
    int Top;
    String Label;
    String Text;

    public TextBox(int x, int y, String lbl)
    {
        Left = x;
        Top = y;
        Label = lbl;
        Text = "";
    }

    public boolean active()
    {
        return Selected;
    }
```

```java
public void clear(Graphics g)
{
    Selected = false;
    g.setColor(Color.white);
    g.fillRect(Left + 126, Top + 1, 274, 20);
    g.setColor(Color.black);
    g.setFont(new Font("Courier", Font.BOLD, 12));
    g.drawString(Text, Left + 130, Top + 15);
    return;
}

public boolean clicked(int x, int y)
{
    if (x < Left + 125) return false;
    if (x > Left + 400) return false;
    if (y < Top) return false;
    if (y > Top + 21) return false;
    return true;
}

public void process(int key)
{
    int n;

    if (key == 8)
    {
        n = Text.length() - 1;
        Text = Text.substring(0, n);
        return;
    }
    if ((key >= 32) && (key <= 127))
    {
        Text = Text + (char) key;
        return;
    }
    return;
}

public void show(Graphics g)
{
    Text = "";
    g.setColor(Color.black);
    g.setFont(new Font("Arial", Font.PLAIN, 12));
    g.drawString(Label, Left, Top + 15);
    g.drawRect(Left + 125, Top, 275, 21);
    return;
}
```

(continued)

```
        public void toggle(Graphics g)
        {
            int x;

            Selected = !Selected;
            if (Selected)
            {
                g.setColor(Color.blue);
                g.fillRect(Left + 126, Top + 1, 274, 20);
                g.setColor(Color.white);
                g.setFont(new Font("Courier", Font.BOLD, 12));
                g.drawString(Text, Left + 130, Top + 15);
                x = (Left + 130) + (Text.length() * 7);
                g.setColor(Color.yellow);
                g.fillRect(x, Top + 15, 7, 2);
            }
            else
            {
                g.setColor(Color.white);
                g.fillRect(Left + 126, Top + 1, 274, 20);
                g.setColor(Color.black);
                g.setFont(new Font("Courier", Font.BOLD, 12));
                g.drawString(Text, Left + 130, Top + 15);
            }
            return;
        }

        public void update(Graphics g)
        {
            int x;

            g.setColor(Color.blue);
            g.fillRect(Left + 126, Top + 1, 274, 20);
            g.setColor(Color.white);
            g.setFont(new Font("Courier", Font.BOLD, 12));
            g.drawString(Text, Left + 130, Top + 15);
            x = (Left + 130) + (Text.length() * 7);
            g.setColor(Color.yellow);
            g.fillRect(x, Top + 15, 7, 2);
            return;
        }

    }


class RadioButton extends Object
{
    boolean Selected;
    int Left;
    int Top;
    String Label;
```

```java
    public RadioButton(int x, int y, String lbl)
    {
        Left = x;
        Top = y;
        Label = lbl;
    }

    public void clear(Graphics g)
    {
        Selected = false;
        g.setColor(Color.white);
        g.fillRect(Left, Top, 18, 18);
        g.setColor(Color.black);
        g.drawOval(Left, Top, 17, 17);
        return;
    }

    public boolean clicked(int x, int y)
    {
        if (x < Left) return false;
        if (x > Left + 17) return false;
        if (y < Top) return false;
        if (y > Top + 17) return false;
        return true;
    }

    public void show(Graphics g)
    {
        g.setColor(Color.white);
        g.fillRect(Left, Top, 18, 18);
        g.setColor(Color.black);
        g.drawOval(Left, Top, 17, 17);
        g.setFont(new Font("Arial", Font.PLAIN, 12));
        g.drawString(Label, Left + 30, Top + 14);
        return;
    }

    public void toggle(Graphics g)
    {
        Selected = !Selected;
        g.setColor(Color.white);
        g.fillRect(Left, Top, 18, 18);
        g.setColor(Color.black);
        g.drawOval(Left, Top, 17, 17);
        if (Selected)
        {
            g.fillOval(Left + 3, Top + 3, 12, 12);
        }
        return;
    }

}
```

(continued)

```java
class CheckBox extends Object
{
    boolean Selected;
    int Left;
    int Top;
    String Label;

    public CheckBox(int x, int y, String lbl)
    {
        Left = x;
        Top = y;
        Label = lbl;
    }

    public boolean clicked(int x, int y)
    {
        if (x < Left) return false;
        if (x > Left + 17) return false;
        if (y < Top) return false;
        if (y > Top + 17) return false;
        return true;
    }

    public void show(Graphics g)
    {
        g.setColor(Color.white);
        g.fillRect(Left, Top, 18, 18);
        g.setColor(Color.black);
        g.drawRect(Left, Top, 17, 17);
        g.setFont(new Font("Arial", Font.PLAIN, 12));
        g.drawString(Label, Left + 30, Top + 14);
        return;
    }

    public void toggle(Graphics g)
    {
        Selected = !Selected;
        g.setColor(Color.white);
        g.fillRect(Left, Top, 18, 18);
        g.setColor(Color.black);
        g.drawRect(Left, Top, 17, 17);
        if (Selected)
        {
            g.drawLine(Left, Top, Left + 17, Top + 17);
            g.drawLine(Left, Top + 17, Left + 17, Top);
        }
        return;
    }

}
```

5F: After you have entered and verified the source code, save it by selecting **Save** from the **File** menu.

Step 6: Create a new folder called *images* under your current project folder. The complete path of the new folder will be */Java-??/Act16/images*. (If you're not sure how to complete this step, please refer back to Step 6 in Activity 12.)

Step 7: Download the graphics image file called **pizza.gif** and save it in the new *images* folder you just created. (Again, if you don't remember exactly how to do this, refer back to Step 7 of Activity 12.)

Step 8: Build and execute your Java applet.

8A: Build the A*ct16* project by selecting **Build Act16** from the **Build** menu. If you entered the Java source file correctly, you should see the message "Act16 - 0 error(s), 0 warning(s)" displayed in the bottom window. If the Visual J++ compiler reports any errors, you will have to find them, correct them, and then repeat Step 8A until all errors are eliminated.

8B: Once your project is completely error free, execute the *Act16* applet by selecting **Execute** from the **Build** menu.

8C: The first time you attempt to execute your applet, Visual J++ will display a dialog box entitled **Information For Running Class**. When this dialog box appears, simply enter **Act16.class** in the **Class file name** box. Then click **OK**. Visual J++ will automatically tell Internet Explorer to load. When the browser has loaded, it will run your newly created applet.

8D: When the applet runs, click on the "Order Now!" button to display the "Virtual Pizza Order Form." Experiment with the form by filling in your name, address, and telephone information. Also try click on the pizza size and pizza topping controls.

Note: The "Submit" button will *not* be active in this activity. You will make this button active in Activity 17.

At first glance, you will only see one new item on the screen, which is the "Order Now!" button located right below the panning marquee. When you click on the button with your mouse, however, you will see what all that new Java code is doing. In fact, let's quickly review the most important parts of the new sections of code.

First, the **Act16** class has several new methods defined, but let's just focus on two of them. The **mouseDown( )** method is called by the browser whenever a mouse click occurs. It is then responsible for determining if the click should be processed by one of the new objects you added to the applet. If so, this method sets an event code that can then be processed within the **run( )** method. The **keyDown( )** method performs a similar function, but it is called by the browser in response to keystrokes rather than mouse clicks. The keystrokes are used in the name, address, and phone number text boxes on the virtual pizza form.

You also added four new classes to the end of the applet source code. They are called **CmndButton**, **TextBox**, **RadioButton**, and **CheckBox**. These classes are responsible for displaying different types of components on the screen and making them respond to user input. The command buttons, for example, are labeled "Order Now!" on the opening screen and "Submit" and "Cancel" on the order form. They respond to mouse clicks and cause some action (or command) to be performed. The text box objects appear on the order form, and they respond both to mouse clicks (for text box selection) and to keystrokes (for entering character data in the fields). Radio buttons are displayed as small circles. Radio buttons are used when only one option from a set of objects may be chosen. Only one option from a set of radio buttons can be active at any one time. The options are said to be **mutually exclusive.** On your order form, radio buttons are used for the pizza size because one size must be selected.

Check boxes display as small squares, and they behave a little differently than radio buttons. Check box options are *not* mutually exclusive. Therefore they can be selected independently of each other. The user is free to choose any combination of one or more check box options (or none of them for that matter). On your order form, check boxes are used for the pizza toppings.

These four objects help make your Java applet interactive and, therefore, useful. With the addition of these classes, you have definitely moved far beyond the point of being a casual beginner and have entered the realm of the serious Java programmer. Take a bow!

Debriefing

In this activity, you reviewed the concept of making your applet interactive — that is, able to respond to user input via the mouse and the keyboard. The **mouseDown( )** and **keyDown( )** methods are the primary means whereby applets can react to these events. In addition, you learned how to declare and define new Java classes to create user-interactive screen objects. In this case, you created objects to implement the "standards controls" called command buttons, text boxes, radio buttons, and check boxes.

Challenge!

If you carefully study the Java source code that implements the user-interactive controls, you will notice that they are not as general purpose as they could be. For example, the **CmndButton** class is only capable of creating a command button that is 120 pixels wide and 30 pixels high. There may be many occasions when you would like to add a command button to a Java applet that is a different size, whether that be bigger, smaller, taller, whatever. To really make sure you have a firm grip on these principles, try modifying the **CmndButton** class definition so that it will support a button of any width or height.

utting Java Images in Motion

In the previous activity, the "Submit" button on the virtual pizza order form was disabled or "grayed out." You will change that in this activity. You will use the "Submit" button to trigger Java animation. What is an animation? Simply put, an animation is a sequence of one or more images that are displayed in such a way that they appear to move on the computer screen. Sometimes animations are very complex, using hundreds or even thousands of images that are displayed at rates of up to 60 frames per second. But don't worry, the animation that you will create is very simple. You will use a single image that will be updated at a rate of 8 frames per second. The algorithm you will use is almost exactly the same as the one you used for the panning marquee in Activity 15. The only difference is that this algorithm displays an image of a pizza delivery van rather than a string of text. Okay, enough talk. Let's get this final activity completed so Senore Appletto's virtual pizza can be delivered!

O b j e c t i v e s :

- Apply motion techniques to images.
- Compare and contrast the similarities between animations and panning marquees.

Step 1: Start Visual J++. If there are any windows open from a previous project, close them.

Step 2: Create a new Java project.

    2A: Select **New** from the **File** menu.

    2B: Click on **Java Project** under the **Projects** tab.

    2C: Enter **Act17** in the **Project name** box.

    2D: Click on the browse button next to the edit box labeled **Location**. Locate your Java-?? folder and click on the **OK** button to select it.

    2E: Now click on the **OK** button at the bottom of the **New** dialog box. Visual J++ will create a new project in your Java-?? folder called *Act17*.

Step 3: Create an HTML file for this project.

    3A: Select the **New** option from the **File** menu.

    3B: Click on the **HTML Page** option under the **Files** tab.

    3C: Enter **Act17.html** as the name of the HTML file in the **File name** box.

    3D: Click on the **OK** button at the bottom of the **New** dialog box. Visual J++ will now create a sample HTML file for you and display it in the right window.

Activity **17** A Java Animation

Step 4: Make changes to your HTML file.

4A: Locate the line of HTML text that reads:

```
<TITLE>Document Title</TITLE>
```

Change the words "Document Title" to "Appletto's Virtual Pizza." The line of HTML text should now read:

```
<TITLE>Appletto's Virtual Pizza</TITLE>
```

4B: Locate the line of HTML text that reads:

```
<!-Insert HTML here ->
```

Replace this line of text with three new lines that read as follows:

```
<APPLET CODE="Act17.class" WIDTH=600 HEIGHT=450>
```

```
Appletto's Virtual Pizza
```

```
</APPLET>
```

Figure A17.1 shows a complete listing of the entire HTML file as it should now appear.

Figure A17.1
HTML Document after
Changes

```
<HTML>
<HEAD>
<META NAME="Generator" Content="Microsoft Developer Studio">
<META HTTP-EQUIV="Content-Type" content="text/html; charset=iso-8859-1">
<TITLE>Appletto's Virtual Pizza</TITLE>
</HEAD>
<BODY>
<APPLET CODE="Act17.class" WIDTH=600 HEIGHT=450>
Appletto's Virtual Pizza
</APPLET>
</BODY>
</HTML>
```

4C: Check your work carefully. After checking the HTML file, save it by selecting **Save** from the **File** menu.

Step 5: Create your Java applet file.

5A: Select **New** from the **File** menu.

5B: Click on **Java Source File** under the **Files** tab.

5C: Enter **Act17.java** as the name of the Java source file in the **File name** box.

5D: Click on the **OK** button at the bottom of the **New** dialog box. Visual J++ will now create an empty Java source code file.

5E: Enter the following Java code *exactly* as it appears in Figure A17.2.

```
import java.applet.*;
import java.awt.*;

public class Act17 extends Applet implements Runnable
{
    final byte ORDERNOW = 11;
    final byte SUBMIT = 12;
    final byte CANCEL = 13;
    final byte NAME = 21;
    final byte ADDRESS = 22;
    final byte PHONE = 23;
    final byte SMALL = 31;
    final byte MEDIUM = 32;
    final byte LARGE = 33;
    final byte PEPPERONI = 41;
    final byte SAUSAGE = 42;
    final byte MUSHROOMS = 43;
    final byte OLIVES = 44;
    final byte PINEAPPLE = 45;
    final byte KEYDOWN = 50;

    boolean PaintFlag;
    String CompanyName;
    Image PizzaImage;
    Thread PizzaThread;
    String MarqueeText;
    int MarqLeft, MarqRght;
    Image BackPage;
    Graphics OffScreen;
    CmndButton OrderNow;
    CmndButton Submit, Cancel;
    TextBox Name, Address, Phone;
    RadioButton Small, Medium, Large;
    CheckBox Pepperoni, Sausage, Mushrooms, Olives, Pineapple;
    byte EventCode;

    public void init()
    {
        CompanyName = "Appletto's Virtual Pizza";
        MarqueeText = "The best pizza in Cyberspace. Order now!";
        MarqLeft = MarqRght = 0;
        BackPage = createImage(600, 450);
        OffScreen = BackPage.getGraphics();
        OrderNow = new CmndButton(240, 400, "Order Now!");
        Name = new TextBox(100, 90, "Customer Name:");
        Address = new TextBox(100, 115, "Street Address:");
        Phone = new TextBox(100, 140, "Phone Number:");
        Small = new RadioButton(100, 220, "Small");
        Medium = new RadioButton(100, 250, "Medium");
        Large = new RadioButton(100, 280, "Large");
        Pepperoni = new CheckBox(350, 220, "Pepperoni");
        Sausage = new CheckBox(350, 250, "Sausage");
        Mushrooms = new CheckBox(350, 280, "Mushrooms");
```

```
        Olives = new CheckBox(350, 310, "Olives");
        Pineapple = new  CheckBox(350, 340, "Pineapple");
        Submit = new CmndButton(150, 400, "  Submit  ");
        Cancel = new CmndButton(330, 400, "  Cancel  ");
        return;
    }

public boolean keyDown(Event e, int key)
{
    if (Name.active())
    {
        if (key == 9)
        {
            EventCode = ADDRESS;
            return true;
        }
        Name.process(key);
        EventCode = KEYDOWN;
        return true;
    }
    if (Address.active())
    {
        if (key == 9)
        {
            EventCode = PHONE;
            return true;
        }
        Address.process(key);
        EventCode = KEYDOWN;
        return true;
    }
    if (Phone.active())
    {
        if (key == 9)
        {
            EventCode = NAME;
            return true;
        }
        Phone.process(key);
        EventCode = KEYDOWN;
        return true;
    }
    return false;
}

public boolean mouseDown(Event e, int x, int y)
{
    if (OrderNow.clicked(x, y)) EventCode = ORDERNOW;
    if (Name.clicked(x, y)) EventCode = NAME;
    if (Address.clicked(x, y)) EventCode = ADDRESS;
    if (Phone.clicked(x, y)) EventCode = PHONE;
    if (Small.clicked(x, y)) EventCode = SMALL;
```

(continued)

```
          if (Medium.clicked(x, y)) EventCode = MEDIUM;
          if (Large.clicked(x, y)) EventCode = LARGE;
          if (Pepperoni.clicked(x, y)) EventCode = PEPPERONI;
          if (Sausage.clicked(x, y)) EventCode = SAUSAGE;
          if (Mushrooms.clicked(x, y)) EventCode = MUSHROOMS;
          if (Olives.clicked(x, y)) EventCode = OLIVES;
          if (Pineapple.clicked(x, y)) EventCode = PINEAPPLE;
          if (Submit.clicked(x, y)) EventCode = SUBMIT;
          if (Cancel.clicked(x, y)) EventCode = CANCEL;
          if (EventCode != 0) return true;
          return false;
     }

     public void paint(Graphics g)
     {
          g.drawImage(BackPage, 0, 0, this);
          return;
     }

     public void run()
     {
          while (true)
          {
               drawIntro();
               repaint();
               while (true)
               {
                    if (EventCode == ORDERNOW)
                    {
                         doCmndButton();
                         break;
                    }
                    drawMarquee();
                    repaint();
                    pause(125);
               }
               drawForm();
               repaint();
               while (true)
               {
                    if (EventCode == KEYDOWN) doTextBox();
                    if (EventCode == NAME) doTextBox();
                    if (EventCode == ADDRESS) doTextBox();
                    if (EventCode == PHONE) doTextBox();
                    if (EventCode == SMALL) doRadioButton();
                    if (EventCode == MEDIUM) doRadioButton();
                    if (EventCode == LARGE) doRadioButton();
                    if (EventCode == PEPPERONI) doCheckBox();
                    if (EventCode == SAUSAGE) doCheckBox();
                    if (EventCode == MUSHROOMS) doCheckBox();
                    if (EventCode == OLIVES) doCheckBox();
                    if (EventCode == PINEAPPLE) doCheckBox();
```

```
                    if (EventCode == SUBMIT)
                    {
                        doCmndButton();
                        doAnimation();
                        break;
                    }
                    if (EventCode == CANCEL)
                    {
                        doCmndButton();
                        break;
                    }
                    pause(125);
            }
        }
    }

    public void start()
    {
        if (PizzaThread == null)
        {
            PizzaThread = new Thread(this);
            PizzaThread.start();
        }
        return;
    }

    public void stop()
    {
        if (PizzaThread != null)
        {
            PizzaThread.stop();
            PizzaThread = null;
        }
        return;
    }

    public void update(Graphics g)
    {
        if (PaintFlag) paint(g);
        return;
    }

    private void loadImage(Image image, String file)
    {
        boolean done;

        PaintFlag = false;
        image = getImage(getCodeBase(), file);
        while (true)
```

(continued)

```
            {
                done = OffScreen.drawImage(image, 100, 80, 400, 200, null);
                if (done) break;
                pause(125);
            }
            PaintFlag = true;
            return;
        }

        private void pause(long ms)
        {
            try
            {
                PizzaThread.sleep(ms);
            }
            catch (InterruptedException ie)
            {
                PizzaThread.stop();
            }
            return;
        }

        private void doAnimation()
        {
            boolean done;
            int left, rght;
            Image van;

            OffScreen.setColor(Color.white);
            OffScreen.fillRect(1, 1, 598, 448);
            repaint();
            PaintFlag = false;
            van = getImage(getCodeBase(), "images/pizzavan.jpg");
            while (true)
            {
                done = OffScreen.drawImage(van, 1, 1, null);
                if (done) break;
                pause(125);
            }
            PaintFlag = true;
            OffScreen.setColor(Color.white);
            OffScreen.fillRect(1, 1, 598, 448);
            OffScreen.setColor(Color.black);
            left = 600;
            while (true)
            {
                rght = left + 252;
                if (rght < 0) break;
                OffScreen.drawImage(van, left, 140, null);
                OffScreen.drawRect(0, 0, 599, 449);
                repaint();
                pause(125);
```

```
                left -= 8;
        }
        return;
}

private void doCmndButton()
{
    if (EventCode == ORDERNOW)
    {
        OrderNow.push(OffScreen);
        OrderNow.disable();
    }
    if (EventCode == SUBMIT)
    {
        Submit.push(OffScreen);
        Submit.disable();
    }
    if (EventCode == CANCEL)
    {
        Cancel.push(OffScreen);
        Cancel.disable();
    }
    repaint();
    pause(500);
    EventCode = 0;
    return;
}

private void doTextBox()
{
    if (EventCode == NAME)
    {
        Name.toggle(OffScreen);
        Address.clear(OffScreen);
        Phone.clear(OffScreen);
    }
    if (EventCode == ADDRESS)
    {
        Name.clear(OffScreen);
        Address.toggle(OffScreen);
        Phone.clear(OffScreen);
    }
    if (EventCode == PHONE)
    {
        Name.clear(OffScreen);
        Address.clear(OffScreen);
        Phone.toggle(OffScreen);
    }
    if (EventCode == KEYDOWN)
    {
        if (Name.active()) Name.update(OffScreen);
        if (Address.active()) Address.update(OffScreen);
```

(continued)

```java
            if (Phone.active()) Phone.update(OffScreen);
        }
        repaint();
        EventCode = 0;
        return;
    }

    private void doRadioButton()
    {
        if (EventCode == SMALL)
        {
            Small.toggle(OffScreen);
            Medium.clear(OffScreen);
            Large.clear(OffScreen);
        }
        if (EventCode == MEDIUM)
        {
            Small.clear(OffScreen);
            Medium.toggle(OffScreen);
            Large.clear(OffScreen);
        }
        if (EventCode == LARGE)
        {
            Small.clear(OffScreen);
            Medium.clear(OffScreen);
            Large.toggle(OffScreen);
        }
        repaint();
        EventCode = 0;
        return;
    }

    private void doCheckBox()
    {
        if (EventCode == PEPPERONI) Pepperoni.toggle(OffScreen);
        if (EventCode == SAUSAGE) Sausage.toggle(OffScreen);
        if (EventCode == MUSHROOMS) Mushrooms.toggle(OffScreen);
        if (EventCode == OLIVES) Olives.toggle(OffScreen);
        if (EventCode == PINEAPPLE) Pineapple.toggle(OffScreen);
        repaint();
        EventCode = 0;
        return;
    }

    private void drawIntro()
    {
        OffScreen.setColor(Color.blue);
        OffScreen.fillRect(0, 0, 600, 450);
        OffScreen.setColor(Color.black);
        OffScreen.drawRect(0, 0, 599, 449);
        OffScreen.setColor(Color.white);
        OffScreen.setFont(new Font("Arial", Font.BOLD, 30));
        OffScreen.drawString(CompanyName, 135, 50);
```

```
            loadImage(PizzaImage, "images/pizza.gif");
            OffScreen.setColor(Color.black);
            OffScreen.drawRect(100, 80, 399, 199);
            OrderNow.enable();
            OrderNow.show(OffScreen);
            return;
        }

    private void drawMarquee()
    {
        int strlen;
        Font f;
        FontMetrics fm;

        f = new Font("Arial", Font.ITALIC, 24);
        fm = getFontMetrics(f);
        strlen = fm.stringWidth(MarqueeText);
        if (MarqRght <= 0)
        {
            MarqLeft = 600;
            MarqRght = MarqLeft + strlen;
        }
        OffScreen.setColor(Color.yellow);
        OffScreen.fillRect(0, 320, 600, 50);
        OffScreen.setColor(Color.blue);
        OffScreen.setFont(f);
        OffScreen.drawString(MarqueeText, MarqLeft, 352);
        OffScreen.setColor(Color.black);
        OffScreen.drawRect(0, 320, 599, 49);
        MarqLeft -= 8;
        MarqRght -= 8;
        return;
    }

    private void drawForm()
    {
        OffScreen.setColor(Color.white);
        OffScreen.fillRect(1, 1, 598, 448);
        OffScreen.setColor(Color.black);
        OffScreen.setFont(new Font("Arial", Font.BOLD, 30));
        OffScreen.drawString("Virtual Pizza Order Form", 135, 50);
        drawFrame("Customer Information", 50, 75, 500, 100);
        Name.show(OffScreen);
        Address.show(OffScreen);
        Phone.show(OffScreen);
        drawFrame("Pizza Size", 50, 200, 225, 115);
        Small.show(OffScreen);
        Medium.show(OffScreen);
        Large.show(OffScreen);
        drawFrame("Pizza Toppings", 300, 200, 250, 175);
        Pepperoni.show(OffScreen);
        Sausage.show(OffScreen);
```

(continued)

```
                    Mushrooms.show(OffScreen);
                    Olives.show(OffScreen);
                    Pineapple.show(OffScreen);
                    Submit.enable();
                    Submit.show(OffScreen);
                    Cancel.enable();
                    Cancel.show(OffScreen);
                    return;
            }

            private void drawFrame(String s, int x, int y, int w, int h)
            {
                    int n;
                    Font f;
                    FontMetrics fm;

                    f = new Font("Arial", Font.BOLD, 12);
                    fm = getFontMetrics(f);
                    n = fm.stringWidth(s);
                    OffScreen.setColor(Color.black);
                    OffScreen.drawRect(x, y, w, h);
                    OffScreen.setColor(Color.white);
                    OffScreen.drawLine(x + 10, y, x + n + 14, y);
                    OffScreen.setColor(Color.black);
                    OffScreen.setFont(f);
                    OffScreen.drawString(s, x + 12, y + 4);
                    return;
            }

    }


class CmndButton extends Object
{
        boolean Enabled;
        int Left;
        int Top;
        String Label;

        public CmndButton(int x, int y, String lbl)
        {
            Left = x;
            Top = y;
            Label = lbl;
        }

        public boolean clicked(int x, int y)
        {
            if (!Enabled) return false;
            if (x < Left) return false;
            if (x > Left + 119) return false;
            if (y < Top) return false;
```

```
            if (y > Top + 29) return false;
            return true;
    }

    public void disable()
    {
        Enabled = false;
        return;
    }

    public void enable()
    {
        Enabled = true;
        return;
    }

    public void push(Graphics g)
    {
        g.setColor(Color.lightGray);
        g.fillRect(Left, Top, 120, 30);
        g.setColor(Color.black);
        g.drawRect(Left - 1, Top - 1, 121, 31);
        g.setColor(Color.gray);
        g.drawLine(Left, Top, Left + 119, Top);
        g.drawLine(Left, Top, Left, Top + 29);
        g.setColor(Color.black);
        g.setFont(new Font("Courier", Font.BOLD, 16));
        g.drawString(Label, Left + 13, Top + 20);
        return;
    }

    public void show(Graphics g)
    {
        Color c;

        g.setColor(Color.lightGray);
        g.fillRect(Left, Top, 120, 30);
        g.setColor(Color.black);
        g.drawRect(Left - 1, Top - 1, 121, 31);
        g.setColor(Color.white);
        g.drawLine(Left, Top, Left + 119, Top);
        g.drawLine(Left + 1, Top + 1, Left + 118, Top + 1);
        g.drawLine(Left, Top, Left, Top + 29);
        g.drawLine(Left + 1, Top + 1, Left + 1, Top + 28);
        g.setColor(Color.gray);
        g.drawLine(Left + 1, Top + 29, Left + 119, Top + 29);
        g.drawLine(Left + 2, Top + 28, Left + 118, Top + 28);
        g.drawLine(Left + 119, Top + 1, Left + 119, Top + 29);
        g.drawLine(Left + 118, Top + 2, Left + 118, Top + 28);
        c = (Enabled) ? Color.black : Color.gray;
        g.setColor(c);
        g.setFont(new Font("Courier", Font.BOLD, 16));
```

(continued)

Building Web Pages with Java Applets   **159**

```
            g.drawString(Label, Left + 12, Top + 19);
            return;
        }

    }

class TextBox extends Object
{
    boolean Selected;
    int Left;
    int Top;
    String Label;
    String Text;

    public TextBox(int x, int y, String lbl)
    {
        Left = x;
        Top = y;
        Label = lbl;
        Text = "";
    }

    public boolean active()
    {
        return Selected;
    }

    public void clear(Graphics g)
    {
        Selected = false;
        g.setColor(Color.white);
        g.fillRect(Left + 126, Top + 1, 274, 20);
        g.setColor(Color.black);
        g.setFont(new Font("Courier", Font.BOLD, 12));
        g.drawString(Text, Left + 130, Top + 15);
        return;
    }

    public boolean clicked(int x, int y)
    {
        if (x < Left + 125) return false;
        if (x > Left + 400) return false;
        if (y < Top) return false;
        if (y > Top + 21) return false;
        return true;
    }

    public void process(int key)
    {
        int n;
```

```java
        if (key == 8)
        {
            n = Text.length() - 1;
            Text = Text.substring(0, n);
            return;
        }
        if ((key >= 32) && (key <= 127))
        {
            Text = Text + (char) key;
            return;
        }
        return;
    }


    public void show(Graphics g)
    {
        Text = "";
        g.setColor(Color.black);
        g.setFont(new Font("Arial", Font.PLAIN, 12));
        g.drawString(Label, Left, Top + 15);
        g.drawRect(Left + 125, Top, 275, 21);
        return;
    }


    public void toggle(Graphics g)
    {
        int x;

        Selected = !Selected;
        if (Selected)
        {
            g.setColor(Color.blue);
            g.fillRect(Left + 126, Top + 1, 274, 20);
            g.setColor(Color.white);
            g.setFont(new Font("Courier", Font.BOLD, 12));
            g.drawString(Text, Left + 130, Top + 15);
            x = (Left + 130) + (Text.length() * 7);
            g.setColor(Color.yellow);
            g.fillRect(x, Top + 15, 7, 2);
        }
        else
        {
            g.setColor(Color.white);
            g.fillRect(Left + 126, Top + 1, 274, 20);
            g.setColor(Color.black);
            g.setFont(new Font("Courier", Font.BOLD, 12));
            g.drawString(Text, Left + 130, Top + 15);
        }
        return;
    }
```

(continued)

```
       public void update(Graphics g)
       {
           int x;

           g.setColor(Color.blue);
           g.fillRect(Left + 126, Top + 1, 274, 20);
           g.setColor(Color.white);
           g.setFont(new Font("Courier", Font.BOLD, 12));
           g.drawString(Text, Left + 130, Top + 15);
           x = (Left + 130) + (Text.length() * 7);
           g.setColor(Color.yellow);
           g.fillRect(x, Top + 15, 7, 2);
           return;
       }

   }


class RadioButton extends Object
{
    boolean Selected;
    int Left;
    int Top;
    String Label;

    public RadioButton(int x, int y, String lbl)
    {
        Left = x;
        Top = y;
        Label = lbl;
    }

    public void clear(Graphics g)
    {
        Selected = false;
        g.setColor(Color.white);
        g.fillRect(Left, Top, 18, 18);
        g.setColor(Color.black);
        g.drawOval(Left, Top, 17, 17);
        return;
    }

    public boolean clicked(int x, int y)
    {
        if (x < Left) return false;
        if (x > Left + 17) return false;
        if (y < Top) return false;
        if (y > Top + 17) return false;
        return true;
    }
```

```java
    public void show(Graphics g)
    {
        g.setColor(Color.white);
        g.fillRect(Left, Top, 18, 18);
        g.setColor(Color.black);
        g.drawOval(Left, Top, 17, 17);
        g.setFont(new Font("Arial", Font.PLAIN, 12));
        g.drawString(Label, Left + 30, Top + 14);
        return;
    }

    public void toggle(Graphics g)
    {
        Selected = !Selected;
        g.setColor(Color.white);
        g.fillRect(Left, Top, 18, 18);
        g.setColor(Color.black);
        g.drawOval(Left, Top, 17, 17);
        if (Selected)
        {
            g.fillOval(Left + 3, Top + 3, 12, 12);
        }
        return;
    }

}


class CheckBox extends Object
{
    boolean Selected;
    int Left;
    int Top;
    String Label;

    public CheckBox(int x, int y, String lbl)
    {
        Left = x;
        Top = y;
        Label = lbl;
    }

    public boolean clicked(int x, int y)
    {
        if (x < Left) return false;
        if (x > Left + 17) return false;
        if (y < Top) return false;
        if (y > Top + 17) return false;
        return true;
    }
```

(continued)

```java
public void show(Graphics g)
{
    g.setColor(Color.white);
    g.fillRect(Left, Top, 18, 18);
    g.setColor(Color.black);
    g.drawRect(Left, Top, 17, 17);
    g.setFont(new Font("Arial", Font.PLAIN, 12));
    g.drawString(Label, Left + 30, Top + 14);
    return;
}

public void toggle(Graphics g)
{
    Selected = !Selected;
    g.setColor(Color.white);
    g.fillRect(Left, Top, 18, 18);
    g.setColor(Color.black);
    g.drawRect(Left, Top, 17, 17);
    if (Selected)
    {
        g.drawLine(Left, Top, Left + 17, Top + 17);
        g.drawLine(Left, Top + 17, Left + 17, Top);
    }
    return;
}

}
```

5F: After you have entered and verified the source code, save it by selecting **Save** from the **File** menu.

Step 6: Create a new folder called *images* under your current project folder. The complete path of the new folder will be */Java-??/Act17/images.* (If you're not sure how to complete this step, please refer back to Step 6 in Activity 12.)

Step 7: Download the graphics image files called **pizza.gif** and **pizzavan.jpg**, and save them in the new *images* folder you just created. (Again, if you don't remember exactly how to do this, refer back to Step 7 of Activity 12.)

Step 8: Build and execute your Java applet.

8A: Build the A*ct17* project by selecting **Build Act17** from the **Build** menu. If you entered the Java source file correctly, you should see the message "Act17 - 0 error(s), 0 warning(s)" displayed in the bottom window. If the Visual J++ compiler reports any errors, you will have to find them, correct them, and then repeat Step 8A until all errors are eliminated.

8B: Once your project is completely error free, execute the *Act17* applet by selecting **Execute** from the **Build** menu.

8C: The first time you attempt to execute your applet, Visual J++ will display a dialog box entitled **Information For Running Class**. When this dialog box appears, simply enter **Act17.class** in the **Class file name** box. Then click **OK**. Visual J++ will automatically tell Internet Explorer to load. When the browser has loaded, it will run your newly created applet.

Congratulations, you have just completed your final Java activity! Let's quickly review the code you added to make the pizza delivery animation work. There are really only two areas to examine.

First, you added the **Submit.enable( )** statement near the end of the **drawForm( )** method to enable the "Submit" command button on the virtual pizza order form. Then you added a few other lines of code to handle the event that is generated when the button is clicked. These new lines of code are located in the **mouseDown( )** method and the **run( )** method.

The bulk of the animation code is in the new method you added called **doAnimation( )**, so let's study this section more closely. First it loads the pizza van image into memory, then it enters a loop to display the image over and over again at different locations. The delay between each display iteration is 125 milliseconds (1/8 of a second), so the image is displayed 8 times per second. The X coordinate is adjusted 8 pixels to the left after each repetition, so the pizza van appears to move across the screen.

Debriefing

In this activity, you learned how to trigger a simple animation sequence with a command button. You also learned how to create an animation by displaying an image over and over again at different locations on the screen. This approach is very similar to the method you used to display a panning marquee. More sophisticated animations can be created by adding more images and by adding additional threads of execution.

Challenge!

Since this is the final challenge of this book, it is only fitting that it be the most difficult, but also the most useful. You have now reached the point where you should be able to start using the concepts you learned while creating Senore Appletto's Web page to create your own Web page. Design a brand new HTML page for a fictitious company. Create a Java applet that does all the things Senore Appletto's applet does. Your new applet should display a company name, an appropriate image, a scrolling message, an order form (with text boxes, radio buttons, check boxes, and command buttons), and a simple animation. When you have completed this challenge, we recommend that you throw yourself a big party!

Glossary

.gif: Graphics Interchange Format. One of the most widely used graphics formats on the World Wide Web. Created by CompuServe.

.htm: A file extension used by DOS and Windows computers to identify HTML documents to Web browsers.

.html: A file extension used by Windows 95 or higher, Macintosh, and UNIX computers to identify HTML documents to Web browsers.

.jpeg: Joint Photographic Expert Group. The Joint Photographic Expert Group was an international committee that defined this standard graphics file format. This graphics format is widely used on the Web.

.jpg: See .jpeg

.txt: A file extension that indicates the file is a text document.

Angle Brackets: Angle brackets identify HTML commands to Web browsers. Angle brackets look like this: < >

Appleto, Senore: The Java pizza person in this book.

AppletWizard: Special Visual J++ tools that create standard source code for common programming problems, saving the programmer time with certain programming tasks.

Applets: Applets are executable programs written for the World Wide Web using the Java programming language. Applet is also a term given to small applications. (See Applications)

Applications: Software programs or executables are often called applications.

ASCII: American Standard Code for Information Interchange. Includes standard characters that all computers can read and understand. They include the letters, numbers, and symbols found on the keyboard, and other characters.

Assembly Language: One of the first programming languages. Considered a lower-level language, assembly is actually closer to machine language than to other high-level object-oriented languages. While hard to learn, assembly has the advantage of increased execution speed. (See Lower Level Languages)

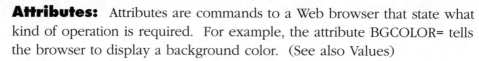

Attributes: Attributes are commands to a Web browser that state what kind of operation is required. For example, the attribute BGCOLOR= tells the browser to display a background color. (See also Values)

AWT: (See Abstract Windowing Toolkit)

Abstract Windowing Toolkit: Also called the Abstract Window Toolkit; includes a set of classes that accomplish various graphics and windowing features in Java.

Binary: A numbering system based on 0 and 1.

Bookmarks: Bookmarks provide Netscape users a way to list their favorite Web pages so they can return to them easily. Internet Explorer users call this feature "Favorites."

Braces: Braces include { and }. They are used to mark the beginning and end of segments or blocks of source code.

Brackets: (See Angle Brackets.)

Browse: On the World Wide Web, browse is another word for surf or search.

Browser: A browser or Web browser is a software tool that searches and displays HTML and other documents and graphics from the Internet and World Wide Web. The most popular browsers are Netscape and Internet Explorer.

Bundled: Bundled means grouped together. If software is bundled with a book, it means the software is provided with the book.

Bytecodes: Java compiles Java source code into bytecodes. Bytecodes are converted and run by the Java-enabled browser.

C++: An object-oriented programming language based on the C programming language.

CGI: Common Gateway Interface. CGI allows users to interact with Web pages. For example, with CGI you can create forms, have Web visitors enter data into the form, and have that data processed. CGI is a recognized standard for interfacing applications, like database programs, with Web servers and Web pages.

Circuits: Miniaturized electrical switches, millions of which can be placed on a computer chip.

Class: (See Classes and Object Oriented Programming)

Classes: Classes are the foundations of object-oriented programming. Classes define objects. Classes must defined. For example, a class that draws a square could be called the square class. Classes are reusable, which means that classes and the objects they create can be used over and over again in other programs or in other parts of the same program.

ClassView: ClassView is an option in Visual J++ that allows you to see all of the classes and methods used in a program in a graphical or visual way.

Close Tags: Close tags end HTML commands. Close tags are easy to spot because of the identifying forward slash as in </CENTER>.

Comments: Comments are placed in source code to inform other programmers how the course code works (See Explanatory Comments) or to remind the programmer of things that still need to be done to fix the source code (See Todo Comments).

Compelling Web Site: A compelling Web site is one that visitors want to visit again and again.

Compiler: A compiler is a software program that converts source code into application software. Java compilers can also convert source code into bytecodes that can be interpreted by a Java-enabled browser.

Compiling: The process of turning source code into applications or applets. (See Compiler)

Cyberspace: A term used to describe the Internet and the World Wide Web.

Debugger: Integrated Development Environments like Visual J++ and Visual C++ have special debugging software that looks through source code to find errors. Debuggers save programmers time finding common problems in source code.

Decimal: A numbering system based on the numbers 1 to 9 and zero.

Developer: Another name for a computer programmer.

Developer Studio: Microsoft's development environment for programmers.

Development Environment: (See Integrated Development Environment)

Directory: A directory is a term used to describe a logical place to save electronic files on computer hard drives, CD's, or diskettes. On the Web, directories are separated by slashes. For example, /swpco in this example is a directory. (See also Subdirectory and Folder.)

http://www.thomson.com/swpco/internet/markweb.html

DOS: Disk Operating System.

Executables: Application software programs and applets are often called executables. On the Windows platform, executables can be seen with an .exe extension in the filename.

Explanatory Comments: These explain to others how the program works and why the programmer wrote the source code a certain way. Explanatory comments answer the question, "Why is this program written in this way?"

Extend: An instruction in Java that adds or extends the attributes or abilities of one class to a new class.

Extensions: Extensions are identifiers for filenames. For example, the extension .htm or .html identifies HTML documents. The file extension .txt often identifies text documents. The extension .doc identifies Word documents and the extension .wpd identifies WordPerfect documents.

FAQ: Internet talk for Frequently Asked Questions.

Favorites: Favorites is the term the Internet Explorer uses for bookmarks or hotlists. (See Bookmarks)

File Extensions: (See Extensions)

Flame: A written rebuke over the Internet.

Folder: A term often used for a directory or subdirectory. A logical place to save files, graphics, and data.

Formatting tags: Formatting tags add interest to Web pages. They include commands that can be compared to word processing commands. Examples include bold <B>, italic<I>, bigger <H1> or smaller <H6> letters; Center <CENTER>, left <LEFT>, and right <RIGHT> justify.

Freeware: Software that anyone can use freely. Freeware can be downloaded from the Internet.

FTP: File Transfer Protocol. FTP is used to transfer files and data from one computer to another on the Internet.

Graphics: Graphics are pictures in an electronic format. The most popular graphics formats on the Web are .gif and .jpeg. (See also .gif and .jpeg)

GUI: Graphical User Interface. GUI simply means pictures or icons are substituted for words on a computer interface. For example, the command CUT is often replaced by a picture of a pair of scissors.

HEX: (See Hexadecimal)

Hexadecimal: A numbering system based on 16 rather than 10. Hexadecimal uses the letters A, B, C, D, E, and F along with numbers 0 to 9 to create new number combinations.

High Level Languages: These include Pascal, C++, Visual Basic, Java, and other languages. Higher level languages use commands and instructions that are easier for the programmer to remember that don't always correspond to the instructions the computer processor

understands. High Level Languages need to be compiled or translated into the kinds of instructions a computer processor understands.

Home Page: A home page is usually the starting page of a Web site. Many people call all Web pages home pages. While not technically correct, every qualified Web surfer understands that both terms are often used interchangeably. (See Web page.)

HTML: (See Hypertext Markup Language.)

HTML Editor: A specialized text editor that allows users to enter HMTL tags quickly and easily.

HTML Tags: (See Tags.)

Hyperlinks: Hyperlinks include both words and/or pictures that are linked or referenced to other Web pages or pieces of Internet information. Hyperlinks send you to new and related information.

Hypertext Links: Hypertext links are words that "link" or send you out to cyberspace for other related Web pages of information. Hypertext links are usually underlined or appear in a different color.

Hypertext Markup Language: The language of the World Wide Web, HTML, uses tags or commands in angle brackets < > to instruct Web browsers how to display documents and graphics.

Import: A Java instruction that brings specified classes into a specific method or class.

Information Superhighway: Another name for the Internet and the World Wide Web.

Integrated Development Environment: An integrated development environment (IDE) is a group of programming software programs and utilities that are specifically designed to help the programmer create applications and applets. IDEs include compilers, debuggers, development wizards, and viewers.

Internet: A world-wide network of networks connecting millions of computers, servers, and computer users together.

Internet Assistant for Word: Created by Microsoft, Internet Assistant is the popular word processing program's HTML editor. Easy to use, Internet Assistant is now bundled with Word or can be downloaded from Microsoft.

Internet Explorer: Microsoft's popular Web browser.

Internet Publisher: Corel WordPerfect's HTML Editor.

Internet Service Provider: An Internet Service Provider (ISP) is a company or organization that provides access to the Internet and World Wide Web. The largest ISP today is America Online or AOL. There are many others, large and small, including Microsoft Network (MSN), Prodigy, and CompuServe.

Interpreter: An interpreter converts bytecodes into run-time programs in Java. Java-enabled browsers have a built-in Java interpreter.

ISP: (See Internet Service Provider)

Java: A programming language adapted to the needs of the Internet and World Wide Web. Java programs for the Web are called applets.

Java-Enabled Browser: A Web browser that has a Java translator capable of running Java applets.

Java Virtual Machine: Java compilers compile Java bytecodes to run on an imaginary machine called the Java Virtual Machine. This machine allows Java applets programmed to a make-believe computer, then the bytecodes are translated to fit the specific computer they are running on by the Java interpreter inside the Java-enabled browser.

JavaScript: Not to be confused with the Java programming language, JavaScript takes advantage of the capabilities of the browser to read tags and commands. JavaScript allows Java-like programs to be written directly into an HTML document.

Libraries: Java and other programming languages have libraries that store classes of all kinds. Class libraries are like public libraries. The best thing is that you don't have to return your copy of a class taken from your class library. No fine will charged.

Linker: A linker links compiled source code to any other classes or files that must be enabled during the compiling process.

Links: (See Hypertext Links and Hyperlinks.)

Lowercase: Lowercase letters are small letters, not CAPITAL LETTERS.

Low Level Languages: These include machine and assembly languages. Low level languages more closely represent the actual processes on the CPU. They are hard for humans to remember, so higher level languages were created.

Machine Language: The earliest of computer languages, machine language talks directly to the binary processes in the CPU. Machine language is made up of 0's and 1's. Machine language is a low level language. (See Low Level Languages)

Method: A method in Java is like a function in C++. A method is a command or a statement in source code that tells the compiler how a class should operate or function.

Microsoft: Software company started by Bill Gates and Paul Allen. With headquarters in Redmond, Washington, Microsoft is responsible for most computer operating systems and a wide variety of software including Windows, Visual C++, Visual Basic, Visual J++, and Microsoft Office Suite.

Net: Short for Internet. (See Internet.)

Netscape: A popular Web browser. Also the name of the company that created the Netscape Navigator software.

Notepad: Text editor found on the Windows operating system. Notepad saves files in a simple text format with a .txt extension.

Objects: An object is a concept in programming. Objects represent something real, like a circle, or a clock, or any other real-world object. Objects are made "real" by the programmer in the form of a class. (See Classes) Classes can be used over and over again. For example, if you have a "circle class," you have a circle object. Every time you use your circle class you create another instance of the circle object.

Object Oriented Programming: Programming based on creating objects in class files which can be reused by other programs. For example, the Graphics class has graphics code that can be used by other programs to create such things as circles, lines, squares, or even to display text.

Open Tags: Tags that start an option or an HTML command. For example the open <TITLE> tag.

PageMill: The first WYSIWYG HTML editor created by Adobe.

Platform: A specific type of computer and operating system is referred to as a platform. For example, Windows computers consist of one platform, Macintosh computers are another platform, UNIX computers are yet another platform.

Platform Independence: An applet is platform independent if it can run on any of different kinds of computer; Macintosh, Windows, or Unix. (See Platform)

Portability: In computer terms, portability is the ability to transfer and translalte software from one computer platform to another. (See Platform)

Post: (See Posting)

Posting: The act of uploading or transferring HTML Web pages to a Web server to be displayed on the World Wide Web. Pages are normally uploaded using FTP or File Transfer Protocol. FTP is to the Internet what the Copy feature is on your computer operating system software.

Programmer: Someone who writes and creates computer software programs. A programmer is sometimes called a developer.

Project: A project in Visual J++ and Visual C++ includes all the files and classes required to develop an applet or application program.

Public Domain: When pictures and stories are in the public domain, it means that anyone can use them for the purposes for which they were intended. For example, "The Star Spangled Banner" is in the public domain. You can sing or record it without paying someone for the rights to use it. Graphics that are in the public domain can be copied and used on your Web pages.

Refresh: Nearly every browser has a Refresh or Reload feature that allows you to try to load a Web page that may have appeared incompletely or with errors in it. Refresh is the term use with the Internet Explorer browser.

Reload: Nearly every browser has a Reload feature that allows you to reload or refresh a Web page. If a page comes in too slowly or appears with errors in it, Reload or Refresh will try the page again, often fixing the previous problems. Reload is the term used with the Netscape browser.

Reusable: To be able to use repeatedly or over and over again.

Run Native: When an application runs native on a computer it means that it was created especially for that specific kind of computer and operating system.

Search Engine: Software on the Web that allows a user to search for key words or topics. Search engines search Web pages for information related to the words entered into the search request.

Semicolon: Semicolons are used to end or terminate a line of code in Java. In a sense, semicolons are like periods at the end of a sentence.

Server: A special computer that shares files with other computers over a network. Servers serve files or documents and graphics to client computers. Client computers request files or documents and graphics from servers.

Shareware: Software that users can download and try free of charge for a trial period of time. However, if they decide they like the software and want to keep it, they often must pay a fee to continue using it.

Shockwave: Shockwave is software that plays and distributes multimedia programs created with Macromedia Director over the Web. Both Shockwave and Macromedia Director are available through Macromedia at www.macromedia.com.

SimpleText: Text editor found on Macintosh computers. SimpleText saves files in a simple text format.

Slash: A slash is a line that separates file and directory names. This is a slash /. There are actually two kinds of slashes a forward slash / and a backward slash \. The Web uses forward slashes /, for example: http://www.thomson.com/swpco/internet/markweb.html

Source Code: The fundamental instructions written by a programmer that are later compiled into application programs or applets are called source code. All executable programs in Java and C++ start out as source code.

Source Code Editor: Source code editors can be found in Integrated Development Environments. They allow programmers to enter programming instructions. The best source code editors are visual; they color-code various parts of the source code syntax the programmers see where errors have possibly been made.

Starting Tags: Starting tags appear in every HTML document and include the following tags in the following order: <HTML><HEAD><TITLE></TITLE></HEAD><BODY></BODY></HTML>

Studio-JPlus: The website for this and other Java texts can be found at studio-jplus.com.

Subdirectory: A subdirectory is a term used to describe a directory or folder inside another directory of folder. Subdirectories are logical places to save electronic files on computer hard drives, CDs, or diskettes. On the Web, subdirectories are separated by slashes. In the example below, /internet is a subdirectory in the /swpco directory. http://www.thomson.com/swpco/internet/markweb.html (See also Directory and Folder)

SUN Microsystems: The computer company that created the Java programming language.

Syntax: The way instructions are entered into source code is called syntax. Syntax is like language grammar rules. For example, just as every sentence needs a noun, every Java program needs a method.

Syntax Error: If you key an instruction incorrectly into your source code you get a syntax error.

Tags: Tags are used in HTML to signal commands and instructions to Web browsers. Tags mark a document in ways that instruct the browser to display the document in specific ways. Tags appear in angle brackets like this: <TAG>.

Text Editor: A text editor like Notepad or SimpleText allows the user to type words and text characters and save them in a text file format. Source code can be written into a text editor, then transferred to the Java compiler.

Text Export: Saving a file as a text file requires the host software to perform a translation of the file into a text format, often called a text export.

Text File: A file saved in a text format, usually with extensions such as .txt, .htm, or .html.

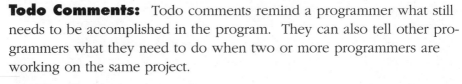

Todo Comments: Todo comments remind a programmer what still needs to be accomplished in the program. They can also tell other programmers what they need to do when two or more programmers are working on the same project.

Toolbars: Toolbars are made up of buttons, usually at the top of most software programs. Normally a series of icons or pictures, toolbar buttons give you one-click access to commonly used software commands. For example, nearly every software browser has a Stop button on its toolbar.

Translator: Translates Java bytecodes into software the specific computer and its operating system can understand. Translators are found in Java-enabled browsers.

Truncated Filenames: Filenames, particularly in DOS, are often shortened. These truncated filenames may change a filename like GETTYSBURGADDRESS.TEXT to GETTYSBE.TXT.

Uniform Resource Locator: A Uniform Resource Locator or URL is an address used to find documents on the World Wide Web. A URL can be a series of words or numbers separated by periods and slashes. For example: http://www.thomson.com/swpco/internet/markweb.html or http://159.91.6.2/MyStuff/file.html

UNIX: Important mainframe computer operating system and computer platform. UNIX computers are widely used on the Web because they are fast and reliable. UNIX was created by Bell Labs and many versions of it are free.

Uppercase: Uppercase letters are CAPITAL LETTERS.

URL: (See Uniform Resource Locator.)

Values: Values define attributes. For example, many color values can be defined for the attribute BGCOLOR=. Words like WHITE, or RED or BLUE can be values. Values can also be numbers, like FFFFFF for White, FF0000 for Red, and 0000FF for Blue.

Variables: Variables allow change within a program. For example, you can change colors by changing the color variables. You can speed up or slow down an animation by changing the speed or timing variable for the animation.

Viewer: A viewer allows a programmer to view software applications once they have been compiled. A Web browser like Internet Explorer or Netscape can serve as a Java applet viewer.

Visual C++: Microsoft's C++ development environment.

Visual J++: Microsoft's Java development system.

Web: (See World Wide Web)

Web Browser: (See Browser)

Web Document: (See Web page)

Web Page: A Web page is a page of information created in HTML and displayed on the World Wide Web. Also called a home page or a Web document.

Web Server: A special computer that contains Web pages that Web users can access and view. (See also Server)

Web Site: A series of interrelated Web pages on a particular topic constitutes a Web site. Companies like Microsoft have extensive Web sites dedicated to their company products and services. Schools can also have Web sites or collections of Web pages created by their students.

Webmaster: A Webmaster is the guardian of a Web server. These people create and manage Web pages, Web sites, and Internet services.

Word: A very popular word processing program written and owned by Microsoft. Word has a built-in or "bundled" HTML Editor called the Internet Assistant.

WordPerfect: A very popular word processing program owned Corel that has a built in or "bundled" HTML Editor called the Internet Publisher.

World Wide Web: A series of computers that use and understand the HTTP or Hypertext Transfer Protocol. These computers transmit HTML documents to Web users around the world.

Wraparound: Text editors and word processors with a wraparound feature will automatically shift the text down when the end of the line is reached. Some text editors do not have a wraparound feature, so the user must press Enter or Return at the end of each line of text.

WWW: Acronym for the World Wide Web. (See World Wide Web)

WYSIWYG: What You See Is What You Get. WYSIWYG approximates on the computer screen what will result in real life. For example, when typing a letter, a WYSIWYG word processing program will display on the monitor what will be printed on a page.

Index